# you deserve better

# y☺u deserve better

**An imperfect guide to
finding your happiness**

Anne-Marie

First published in Great Britain in 2021 by Orion Spring
an imprint of The Orion Publishing Group Ltd
Carmelite House, 50 Victoria Embankment
London EC4Y 0DZ

An Hachette UK Company

1 3 5 7 9 10 8 6 4 2

Copyright © AM Biznus Ltd
Illustrations by Anne-Marie

A CIP catalogue record for this book is
available from the British Library.

ISBN (Hardback) 978 1 3987 0741 2
ISBN (eBook) 978 1 3987 0743 6
ISBN (Audio) 978 1 3987 0744 3

## CREDITS

'Be patient with yourself and the world'

**– Dr Charlie Howard**

# Contents

# Before we get started . . .

This is how my story starts: Once upon a time I couldn't leave the house because of anxiety.

I couldn't even answer the front door to collect a takeaway. I'm serious – I was so scared and worried about what other people thought of me that I couldn't do it. I'd be overwhelmed with anxiety about what the person behind the door would think. Anxiety had turned me into a hermit and I was just afraid of, well . . . everything.

I know it sounds mad, but this was only a few years ago: the same period when I would get up on stage and sing to massive crowds, with thousands of people looking at me. But for some reason, that felt different. Even though everyone was watching me perform, I was able to put it in a separate part of my brain and I knew they weren't thinking about my personality, or judging me like that – it was just about the music. So in those moments when I was up there singing my heart out, all those anxieties that wrecked my life at home didn't matter. It was when I came off stage that the nightmare started again.

The other day, I was clearing out my room and I found an old magazine interview I did a few years ago. I read the first bit but then put it down – I didn't want to read on. It was horrible. The first bit said something like 'Anne-Marie doesn't feel like she belongs here,' and I was like, *Rah, I was in THAT place*. Reading that first line instantly took me back there: that dark place where I didn't feel good about anything in my life. I looked at the pictures too alongside the article and thought, *God, I didn't know who I was at all, then.*

Back in those days, a big part of the cause of my anxiety was that I had massive imposter syndrome – that feeling that you shouldn't be in the position that you are. It's when you believe you're there because of a mistake, and that people are gonna find you out, that you don't deserve your place. My imposter syndrome was so bad that I even felt cringe when anyone would ask for my autograph. Despite having released a debut album that went platinum, been nominated for Brit awards, and had top five singles, I'd be like *Why do you want my autograph? I'm not anyone.* I didn't get it at all.

The result of imposter syndrome is that I was filled with self-doubt and shame about who I was, and what I looked like. And I turned that onto other people, too: I'd be angry all the time, flippant, very reactive and would NEVER believe anyone if they complimented me – I just thought they were lying. And that messed up all of my relationships, because I was constantly in a battle.

*But really, I was in a battle with myself.*

Looking at that magazine now got me thinking: what if I was asked the same set of questions now? Would I give the same answers? Nah, I know that my answers would be completely different.

*Because what I've gone through in the past couple of years has changed me completely.*

Weirdly, everything shutting down when the COVID-19 pandemic hit in 2020 helped me sort out my brain. I was so close to quitting (honestly, really close), thinking that it was music that was making me unhappy. But then lockdown happened, music and my career were removed from my life, and I found I was still unhappy. It was me. Through everything I've done and tried since then though, I've managed to get out of that place – that place where I was battling with myself. I've been on a massive journey of self-discovery: through therapy, through reading, through talking, through learning so much about myself and about what's really behind all my anxieties.

I'm a different person now. I'm happier (and I'm nicer, too!) Every detail of my life is better because I've worked on myself. I can get out of the house, I can walk somewhere new alone, I can chat to people easily on Zoom (OK, I still struggle to answer the phone, but I'm working on that!) I've got so much more space in my head because I'm not obsessing and anxious.

Now, I'm not saying I know it all! I'd be the first person to say I don't have all the answers. But I've learned a lot, and I want to share what I've learned with you.

Because I deserve better than how I treated myself and you deserve better too.

*We ALL deserve better.*

Everything can change and YOU can change it. It's totally possible that if you work on yourself and you make the decision to change, one day you will feel completely different to the way you do right now. Because if I can do it, you definitely can. I used to blame everything the whole time on other people but now I understand that it's not about other people making you feel that way, it's about how you feel about yourself. You have to take responsibility for your emotions. Other people don't make you feel anything – you control your reaction and outcome. You are in control of everything.

And by the way, everyone is struggling with something. EVERYONE. It doesn't matter how amazing their life looks on the surface, how incredible their Instagram images are, how rich they are, blah blah. There will always be something that they're struggling with, no matter how big or small it may be. We need to help each other out, talk about the things we're ashamed of, to lift each other up.

So, in this book, I want to talk to you about everything I've been through, so that it can help you too. I'll tell you my story – my successes, my failures. My highest points and my lowest. My moments of f**k-off pain and moments of f**k-it joy. My total revelations – the things I've learned.

I wanna touch as many lives as possible with my music, and with this book, I wanna open up as many conversations as possible about mental health.

Now, let's be clear, I CAN'T FIX PEOPLE – this isn't a magic solution. Often, those things in magazines that say, 'do this *one* thing and you'll feel better' **don't work**. What I've found instead is that it's really helpful for people to talk. And that's my gift to you. If I can open up lots of conversations about your mental health, your brain's health, then I've done something good.

Because do you know what? However s**t things might feel, it's not the end. It never is. You can start afresh. You CAN make that choice. A new fight, a new friendship, a new haircut, for f**k's sake. Whatever it is. Wake up, feel powerful and make a choice to be the happiest version of you that you can be.

Thanks for coming with me on this journey,

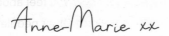

Anne-Marie xx

## A personal video message from me

If you scan the QR code below (using the camera on your smartphone), you'll be able to watch an exclusive video message from me to you! I'm gonna put some more throughout the book, so keep an eye out x

# THE RANDOM FEELINGS GUIDE TO *YOU DESERVE BETTER*!

If you're feeling embarrassed, go to page 30

If you're feeling s**t, go to page 43

If you're feeling sad, go to page 67

If you're feeling shame, go to page 76

If you're feeling lonely, go to page 87

If you're feeling heartbroken, go to page 122

If you're feeling stressed, go to page 162

If you're feeling unmotivated, go to page 166

If you're feeling unconfident, go to page 192

If you're feeling insecure, go to page 212

So, use this book however it works for you – there are NO RULES.
The only thing I'm gonna insist on is that you open up your mind.
You can start letting things out whichever way works for you. It's
simply about being honest about ourselves, and we're gonna start
right now.

We're all a mixture of so many emotions and we can feel a billion
different things in one day. I want you to read this book however
you want to – you can go from beginning to end, or maybe just
read each section individually, whenever you feel like it, in whatever
order. Or, if you're feeling a particular emotion and need a bit of a
boost, you can flick unconventionally through it by going to random
pages . . .

# PART 1

# Let's Talk About You

**O**K, so I'm gonna kick off by getting deep into our emotions. How we can learn to understand ourselves better. To *love* ourselves. Because before we can ask and expect others to treat us better, we need to treat ourselves better. And it all begins with talking, and talking really honestly.

I never used to talk about how I felt. What went on inside me – all my sadness, my insecurities and fears. What I thought about myself as a person and how I looked. I was full of anxieties and negative thoughts, but I kept everything locked down inside, and pretended I was fine. A lot of that attitude came from a really s**t time during my teens, which I'll tell you about a bit later on.

But I know now that I should have opened up – if I had told just one person about what was going on in my brain, whether that was someone in my family or a friend, or even a stranger, things could have got better. They could have helped me see what was really going on, put everything in perspective and reassured me that I was a good person. They could've stopped me feeling so s**t about myself and helped me look at everything rationally.

*One of the biggest reasons why
I didn't open up about my feelings
was embarrassment.*

I felt massively ashamed about my emotions. As if I shouldn't have them, and it was better to pretend everything was OK. Look, here's Anne-Marie, she's really popular and happy, nothing to worry about here!! It was total crap and just made me feel worse deep inside.

The problem was also that I didn't even acknowledge to myself how I felt (so definitely couldn't be truthful to someone else about how I was feeling!) I now know that being aware of your feelings is the start of being able to understand them better and make a change.

## Why I'm being truthful now

But now, thanks to everything I've gone through, I'm the total opposite. I've flipped around and now I let everything out! Now you can't stop me sharing my feelings. And because of that, I am so much happier, for so many reasons. I've realised how important it is to be able to connect with your emotions, and have some way of letting things out. So in this section, I'm gonna talk about all the stuff that goes on inside us – from how we think about our bodies, to looking after ourselves and how we relate to the people that are important to us. By understanding what's happening inside us better, we'll be laying the foundations and strength for us to go out into the world and be the best versions of ourselves we can be.

I know that I'm making myself vulnerable by opening up so much. And I could have chosen to not say anything, ever. I could have been the total opposite and been really closed-off, but I choose to speak up, because it makes *me* happier. It's who I am. As soon as I started out as an artist, my whole aim was to try to be myself and to show people exactly who I was – to be authentic. So that's why I'm sharing everything with you now and if you struggle to open up at the moment, don't worry, you'll be able to get to a more truthful place too.

## Making 'mental health' less scary

If I'm honest, the words 'mental health' used to be really scary to me. It's the word 'mental' in there that used to make me freak out, I mean . . . who decided to call it that! Bit of a jarring word. But I want people to realise that it's not scary, it's just your f**ing brain! It's your brain, and you've got to look after it.

*You look after your heart, you look after your lungs, you look after your stomach, you need to look after your brain, too.*

So if, like me, you find the phrase 'mental health' totally terrifying, then don't worry – you're not alone! All it means is that you're prioritising looking after your brain just as you look after your physical health. In lots of ways, it's harder to take care of because when you break your arm, you *know* you've broken your arm and everyone can see it, and they all want to help. If you're having a crappy day and you feel sad, it can be harder for people to notice and it's also often harder for them to know how to help.

Because mental health is in many ways invisible, I'd like you to promise me that from this point on, you'll try not to hide your feelings – don't feel embarrassed or ashamed, the way I used to. You're allowed to have your feelings, whatever they are – whether you're feeling strong and confident, or completely rubbish. Dealing with the stuff that goes on inside us is SO IMPORTANT because if we don't, it only comes back to bite us later on.

I'm not 100 per cent happy all of the time – of course not! Because our emotions are weird, unpredictable things, and although I feel SO much better than I used to, I still have s**t days. Days when everything feels crud, even though everything might go the same way as it does on a day where I feel amazing. So, to show you just how important your mental health is (and how it's just an everyday part of life), on the next page let's look at two versions of a normal day for me and how I react depending on how I'm feeling.

## GOOD DAY

9 a.m. **burn my toast** – shrug and put another slice in

11 a.m. **read a bad comment on Twitter** – laugh and ignore it

3 p.m. **get my baggy t-shirt caught in the door handle** – unhook it and get on with stuff

7 p.m. **food delivery is 40 mins late** – doesn't matter, I can watch another ep of *The Sopranos* to pass the time!

# BAD DAY

9 a.m. **burn my toast** – scream and cry a little bit

11 a.m. **read a bad comment on Twitter** – cry some more, what they're saying is true, I am ugly, people are horrible

3 p.m. **get my baggy t-shirt caught in the door handle** – shout 'REALLY SATAN!?', be annoyed for the rest of the day, the universe really does hate me

7 p.m. **food delivery is 40 mins late** – complain five times to the restaurant, shout at everyone and everything, eat some sweets in the meantime, when the food comes I'm full of sweets and feel sick, *yay*.

I woke up, look in the mirror today, yeah /
Got so many things that I wanna change

# Dealing with negative body image and learning to love myself

**W**hen I was little I didn't worry about my appearance. Like all kids, my life wasn't about that. Instead, my world revolved around my family, playing on my Game Boy, going to the arcades and being that annoying person who wouldn't get off the dance machine, throwing dressing-up parties with my friends, watching *Pimp My Ride* on TV, and doing loads of musical theatre.

I started dancing at the age of two. Not because I was some kind of prodigy – I just think my mum and dad wanted to get me out of the house! On Saturdays my older sister, Sam, was already going to a dance school near where we lived in Essex, and I wanted to go with her. So, practically as soon as I could walk, I was there. I didn't really do much, all I remember is standing there with people pointing at me and talking about how young I was. In most of the shows we did I was normally the kid that fell over or wouldn't walk off the stage in time (those clips definitely could've got me £250 from *You've Been Framed*).

The teachers at the dance school noticed that I could sing in tune, so they signed me up to the in-house agency, which put kids up for auditions for TV, films and theatre. They put me forward for my first audition when I was six – the role of Little Eponine in the musical *Les Misérables* – and I got the part. My first ever performance took place the day after my seventh birthday (my sister's birthday) and was on London's West End stage! It was incredible. Looking back I think, *What the f\*\*k – how could I have been doing that at that age?* But at the time I had NO concept of how massive it was. And to be honest I was just really excited about getting the time off school.

## First performances and feeling free

I remember having the best time. I was the youngest, smallest Little Eponine they'd ever had, so they had to make a new dress to fit me. All the other costumes were ragged and messed up, because the show was set among the poor people during the French Revolution, but not mine. I had the amazing, beautiful new dress – ugh, I loved that! And I loved performing, I didn't feel scared at all.

It wasn't until I got a new role on the show when I was a little bit older – Little Cosette – that I had to sing in front of hundreds of people. I sang a song called 'Castle on a Cloud', and all of a sudden, I felt a strange new feeling in my belly. When I was at the side of the stage I grabbed hold of my chaperone Sarah's hand. I told her I had a weird feeling in my stomach and I didn't know what it was. She told me it was nerves, but that she could fix it! She mimed getting an imaginary zip and pretended to unzip my belly and said, 'That's all the butterflies coming out now.' And then she pretended to zip me back up – it worked! I felt better and trotted off on stage.

## Starting to become more self-conscious

All throughout that time – even while I was performing in front of audiences – I never worried about what I looked like. I was confident and happy. The first time I remember worrying about how I looked was when I was about ten. At that age, I had really bad teeth. I eventually had braces, but before that my teeth were all over the place. They went backwards, upwards, across, any direction they felt like. But in junior school, that meant that kids – actually it was a couple of boys in particular – started taking the mick out of me.

From that moment onwards, I made the decision that what you looked like was directly linked to how much you got picked on. I figured that they were being horrible to me just because my teeth weren't nice and that if I'd had good teeth, they wouldn't have been like that. That was the first experience I had of caring what I looked like.

*I started to equate looking good with people being nice to you . . . and it only got worse from then on.*

21

Around the same time, I started to become aware that other kids had more money than us. My dad was a welder and my mum was a dinner lady at my school back then, although she became a nursery nurse looking after kids with dyslexia and autism later on. So, they had normal jobs like loads of other families, but it meant we didn't have tons of money going spare. They spent any extra money they had on my karate lessons and dance school.

I didn't use to care that we didn't have much money, and now I know it's not a bad thing at all – I'm really proud of my parents. But once I got into secondary school, I started to be bothered by not being able to buy expensive clothes and brands like other kids at my school. I used to go to charity shops with my dad and I'd find an amazing tracksuit and pair of trainers. I'd be so excited to wear them to school, but when people saw what I was wearing, they would cuss me out because they weren't a massive, cool brand like other people had. I went from feeling on top of the world in my new clothes to feeling embarrassed about them. And it also started to feed into that perception I was developing, that *oh, you need to have money, too, for people to be nice to you.*

*From being really un-self-conscious about how I looked, I had suddenly become massively obsessed with it, and with what other people thought of me.*

In my mind, I started to think, *OK, this is what you need to do to be liked. You need to have the right appearance and more money.*

## Stronger on the outside, but not on the inside

But while these negative thoughts were developing, I also started karate as a hobby. I loved it straight away because I picked it up really quickly. (And who doesn't like something that they're good at?) Not only that, but naturally I was someone who wanted to impress people ALL the time and make them like me, so it made my day when I'd hear my karate instructor say, 'Anne-Marie's a natural' to everyone else in the class. I f**king loved that, so I wanted to do even better. I stayed later, I trained harder. That was it for me – I wanted to be the best.

I trained all the time, after school and every weekend, and got all my belts. Karate made me feel confident, strong and hyper-aware of everyone's movements around me, ready to whack out some karate if needed. I did really well, winning the gold in the Shotokan Karate Association World Championships in 2002. I carried on all throughout my teens, winning more world championships and being dedicated to karate until I was about nineteen. It was my life.

All this outward stuff – these things that I was doing – started to become the role I played. My reputation. In my family, I became 'the sporty successful one that was good at everything', and my family always spoke about me in that light. I really took it upon myself to become the person who I thought they would be most proud of – I adore my family, so what they think really matters to me.

My grandad, BFG, my mum's dad, had this story that he used to tell pretty much everyone we met. It was about when I was around six and he took me and Sam down to the basketball court to play a game. I was still too short to properly play, but apparently I stayed there for hours and hours trying to get the ball in the hoop. I just wouldn't give up.

He used to speak about me in this way to everyone from when I was really little – like I was someone who would keep going until I was the best I could be. He was really proud of me for that, but once I grew up a bit, that determination started to come from a different place. I no longer found my motivation from wanting to be better myself; instead I thought that if I was really good at a sport then people could talk about me in that way, rather than focusing on my appearance or what I could afford to wear.

## THINGS I HADN'T LEARNED YET . . . BUT ARE SO TRUE

People pleasing hides
the real you

Confidence isn't 'they will
like me' confidence is
'I'll be fine if they don't'

Maybe, true happiness is when
we are happy with ourselves

## My weird world of eating habits

Although I was a really sporty teenager, I used to eat SO BAD. I didn't know much about what foods were good or bad for you, so I just ate whatever I wanted. But what I wanted was very, very limited. Get ready – this is what I used to eat on a normal day:

**Breakfast:** peanut butter on toast
**Lunch:** cream cheese sandwiches, a Babybel and crisps
**Dinner:** two more cream cheese sandwiches

And that's it. Every single day. Can you believe it? Loads of dairy, lots of carbs, no meat or fish, no fruit (apart from every now and then) and DEFINITELY no vegetables. I mean, I was really stubborn. I didn't try my first fresh tomato until I was twenty-four! Occasionally I'd eat something different – my family would get Indian and Chinese takeaways – but even then I would really limit my choices. For a Chinese meal, I'd get plain noodles with a strict NO BEAN SPROUT rule, topped with sweet and sour sauce. *Fancy.*

I think a lot of this weird attitude I had to food came from my phobia of vomit. From a really young age I was absolutely terrified of it: me being sick, other people being sick. It controlled my life. It would command where I would sit on a bus, plane or any type of transport. I'd sprint out the house if someone was ill on TV (even the fake sick on hospital TV shows like *Casualty*). It even got to the point where I'd flinch and run away when someone coughed. It was, and still, is very stressful.

Because of this fear, I didn't want anything in my belly that would possibly make me ill, or give me food poisoning. So I limited what I ate to super-plain foods.

*It wasn't healthy, in any way, to live like that.*

But I just carried on happy as Larry, eating my cheese sandwiches.

## Becoming fixated on how I looked

When I was a young teenager, my weird eating habits didn't affect me. I wasn't overweight and didn't have any health problems so I thought *whatever*. I was naturally skinny, and that helped my social life when I was around twelve and thirteen, because at the kind of school I went to, it felt like you 'had' to be skinny to be popular. Things were really good for me then: I felt liked because I was good at sport, and I was already doing West End musicals, which was pretty cool. I was happy.

But things went really bad when I got a bit older, and started having issues with friends and boys. From being one of the popular crew, I became a total outcast who everyone hated. It was awful. My life at school was horrific. It had a massive effect on all parts of my life, too – not just on my self-esteem, but how I dealt with things emotionally, and also how I started to think about myself and my body.

I started to notice more and more people saying things about how I looked. I didn't have any boobs, so the boys started taking the piss out of my flat chest and calling me 'Ironing Board'. Before that I didn't care, because I was young and sporty and it didn't really matter to me. But once they started saying that, I became really embarrassed about it, and started wearing padded bras, then I'd wear a padded bra over the padded bra and so on. I also remember hearing one girl at school complaining about her body, saying, 'I've got such big hips and I don't want them.' And for some reason, that really stayed with me. The thought was fixed into my head, *Oh f\*\*k, well, you'd better not have big hips.* It was such a small comment and it could have been just a passing nothing to someone else, but it stayed with me, and I couldn't let it go.

## My damaging quest to be skinny

After I finished my GCSEs, I went to college to study performing arts. I started hanging around with people who smoked weed, I wouldn't turn up to classes and began eating more beige junk food. Eventually, I also stopped doing all my sport. I remember one day I bumped into someone who'd known me from back at school and he was really shocked at how I'd changed. He said, 'Oh, you're looking *healthy*' but in that backhanded way that meant I'd stacked on weight. That comment really got to me, obviously. So, like with the other things I'd heard other people say about their bodies, I took it in.

I stopped eating properly. I got really skinny, unhealthily so. Not many people seemed to notice, but weirdly someone who did say something was the mum of this boy I was going out with at eighteen. She'd noticed that I didn't eat when I was at their house. So every time I was there, she'd make me eat some tinned beans and sausages. Ew. Bless her.

Although his mum was caring, this boyfriend I had was the worst person in the world for my self-esteem. We'll call him Matthew, and he completely emotionally f**ked me. I was in awe of him, as he was academically intelligent, but he made me feel like poo. He'd say things like 'Are you really gonna wear that lipstick?' or 'You'd look better in a jumper.' These don't sound that bad now I'm writing them out, but they were such damaging things to hear – especially from someone who was meant to care about how I felt. After these comments, I didn't feel comfortable wearing dresses or lipstick.

*It's important to understand that emotionally abusive language doesn't always sound abusive.*

Matthew always made me look crap because he didn't want anyone else to fancy me. We eventually broke up, thank god, but I'd been with him for a few miserable years.

Looking back at this time in my life, which was such a low point, I think my not eating thing was about control. I knew my boyfriend was cheating on me, I didn't have many friends and getting random comments from old school mates on my appearance didn't help either. I couldn't control what people were saying about me, so that's what I did to control some part of my life.

For the next few years, I carried on absorbing all the negative things I'd hear around me. In my early twenties, my music career started to take off, and I was working with my first management label. I met a stylist and asked him what kinda stuff he thought I should wear. He made me spin around in front of him and said, 'You need to lose weight there,' pointing to my hips. I honestly think my jaw dropped. *I could not believe* this stranger said that to me. It took me right back to school. If only he knew the negative talk I was telling myself. Maybe he wouldn't have said it, or maybe he still woulda, arsehole.

## BUSTING BODY MYTHS

> It's total bollocks that there is one 'perfect' type of body shape. THERE IS NO SUCH THING!

> Don't ever base your self-esteem on the sizes in clothing shops – you can be a size 10 in one shop and a size 14 somewhere else. So, basically, it's meaningless!

> Don't surround yourself with people that judge others for their size or looks – and don't be that person, either.

> You are *never* going to change your natural body size, so embrace it. Love it.

> We are all totally individual people, with individual shapes that are programmed by our genetics. Some people are taller, some are shorter. Some are curvier, some are leaner. It's what makes the world such an exciting place . . .

> All shapes and sizes are beautiful. Appreciate your body for what it does for you. It looks after you, so look after it.

## Slowly shifting my mindset

Since breaking up with Matthew, while weight was very much still on my mind, things had got a bit better and I'd started to eat some different stuff. My friend Claire was amazing during this time, and did her best to make me feel better, but my diet was still really limited and I continued to eat cream cheese sandwiches. She did try to help me give other foods a go but apart from that, I'd eat things like chicken nuggets and pizza, bread and peanut butter. My plate would be *beige* and I carried on existing on processed food.

However, my poor diet started to not just be bad for my health but also to affect my life in other ways. At twenty-two I began touring with the band Rudimental, travelling all over the world to sing at gigs. In the evenings, they'd always go out to restaurants and eat these amazing, exciting foods from different cultures and I would literally sit in my hotel room and eat a Caesar salad – wherever I was around the world. I mean, *What were you doing, Anne-Marie?* I could have had any food I wanted, from all these amazing countries! But instead, nope, there I am, sitting on my bed eating my Caesar salad night after night. (I still f\*\*king love a Caesar salad, though!) Through these years of touring with them

*I started to shift my perception of food. I realised how important it was at bringing people together,*

and how my food issues meant I could never really enjoy those moments with them. I was missing out big time. FOMO.

## Still trying to be something I wasn't

Going on tour with Rudimental opened my eyes to a different approach to body size, too. I'd been obsessed with being thin, but I started to notice that the girls they found attractive were curvy. They liked a totally different body shape to the skinny 'ideal' I'd been pursuing.

Of course, me being me, I took that on board 110 per cent and totally changed my approach overnight. I was like *OK, now I want to be curvy*, so I started buying pills off the internet that made me put *on* weight. I know, I know. I mean, what the hell, it was ridiculous (and dangerous). But that was my aim, to be curvy and to have a big bum. I flipped completely in the other direction, like a bloody pancake. But I still wasn't happy because I was still trying to be something I wasn't.

Taking those pills made me feel crap, too. They made me feel so heavy all the time, like I didn't want to move. I had no energy and felt totally UGH. I began to realise that it was because the weight I had on my bones wasn't meant to be there.

*I was trying to force my body – yet again – into a shape it wasn't supposed to be. And I didn't want to feel that way anymore.*

I'd slowly and finally started the process towards thinking more healthily about my body and then a few different things finally transformed my attitude into a healthier, happier one.

## Starting to change the way I thought

The more I wrote music, the more I was able to process what was really going on with me and the way I thought about things. It was a blessing in disguise, really. Because you're sitting in a room going, *What can I write about today?* and that gives you freedom to write anything down and let your subconscious speak. Letting my brain just go in any direction really helped me think about my body in a different way.

I started to realise how amazing my body is. That my body allows me to walk and run and pick things up. To exist. It's keeping me alive. This shift in my thinking made me see myself in a way that wasn't just an object with a shape anymore — that actually, in fact, my body is an amazing machine. It was around the same time I wrote my single 'Perfect To Me'. It's the best song to describe that moment of realisation.

Love every single part of my body / Top to bottom / I'm not a supermodel from a magazine / I'm OK with not being perfect / Cause that's perfect to me /

From that point, I stopped taking the tablets and let my body be the shape it was meant to be. I realised: I'm just going to be my natural size. And I'm just going to accept it and work out and go to the gym because I want to look after it, not because I want to be a certain body shape. Dealing with the shape that I am, naturally. Because that's what's actually important.

This realisation released a lot of stress I had on my shoulders. I was finally letting myself be whatever I was meant to be instead of forcing myself to look like the ever-unreachable person on social media. I finally wasn't trying to look like someone else.

Now, I don't feel like I need to be anything apart from myself. I don't feel *I need to be skinny* or worry if I put on a bit of weight.

*I am the size I am*

and it fluctuates whether I'm working out or if I'm on my bitch of a period. That's what makes it change now – shifts that happen naturally, not because of something I'm doing that's damaging to my health.

Of course, my body confidence can vary massively. When I look in the mirror, I see a different person every day, depending on my mood, what I've eaten the night before, my period, even the weather! If I'm working out all the time, then that's when I'm feeling pukka, like, *Everyone look at me, take a photo of me from whatever angle!* I'll feel great, but then on other days, I can feel really crap, and like, *Why did I have to eat that third burger three days in a row?* Just like anyone else, I have a belly, I have cellulite.

*But even on my bad days I still feel fine - it's not as if I hate myself like I used to.*

I am way more rational about it now! I am just ME.

## SIX THINGS I DO TO SHOW MY BODY I LOVE IT

> Moisturise from head to toe

> Stretch my muscles

> Go for a walk on my own and have a little meditation

> Eat something healthy

> Pop on a face mask – they're the best! Every now and again I surprise my face and give it a little treat.

> Do some face yoga (you can follow along with me in the video below)

## SIX THINGS YOU CAN DO TO SHOW YOUR BODY YOU LOVE IT

1

..................................................................................................

2

..................................................................................................

3

..................................................................................................

4

..................................................................................................

5

..................................................................................................

6

..................................................................................................

## The documentary that transformed the way I ate

Around the same time that I changed how I felt about my body, when I was twenty-seven, I watched a programme called *What the Health* on Netflix. It's not an exaggeration to say that it changed my attitude to food in an incredible way. It's a documentary all about the things we put in our bodies – including antibiotics, cigarettes, meat and dairy products – and the damage they can do to us. It made me understand and consider what we're asking our bodies to do when we put all these things into them.

Up until then, I hadn't really thought about where the meat I ate came from, or what it was doing to not just us, but the world, too. I used to think, *Oh it's just chicken, it doesn't matter.* But watching *What the Health* was a massive eye-opener for me – so much so that I became vegan the very next day.

But – crazy, I know – I STILL didn't eat vegetables! I was stuck without much to eat apart from bread. Luckily peanut butter is vegan and so I ate that for a while. But over time, and because I'd already started to totally shift my attitude towards my body shape, I forced myself to eat every single vegetable available. (Well, apart from beetroot, I am 100 per cent sure I will never like beetroot.) After practising this for a while, I grew to crave vegetables and now I literally love them. I have created a new thing for myself – a healthy and positive habit.

Luckily where I lived in London at the time had loads of different restaurants and shops – from Caribbean food to Vietnamese and Indian food – with loads of vegan options available. So it was quite easy to start trying new things. It helped me with my phobia of being sick, too – being vegan meant I knew I wasn't gonna get food poisoning from undercooked meat! – so it actually freed me up a lot. When I went on my next tour I was able to go out to eat with everyone and just choose the vegan option. I was involved, I wasn't missing out on the social gatherings – and it felt really lovely.

# FOOD THAT MAKES ME FEEL GOOD EVERY TIME:

> Peanut butter and banana toast

> Plantain

> Gherkins

> Vegan burgers

> Chickpea coconut curry

> Little plum tomatoes

> Vegan 'chicken' nugget wraps with barbeque sauce + lettuce

> Vegan wellington

> Smoothie with mango, banana, vegan protein, peanut butter, coconut milk

> Miso aubergines sprinkled with sesame seeds

# FOOD THAT MAKES YOU FEEL GOOD EVERY TIME:

........................................................................

........................................................................

........................................................................

........................................................................

........................................................................

........................................................................

........................................................................

........................................................................

........................................................................

........................................................................

........................................................................

........................................................................

........................................................................

## The life-changing power of eating better

There have been so many amazing benefits to changing what I eat. I never really cooked before (as if you couldn't guess) and now I love experimenting in the kitchen, putting together a nice meal, even if it does take four hours to cook and only ten minutes to eat. I've even started growing my own vegetables on my balcony! During the first lockdown of the pandemic, I grew tomatoes, strawberries, lemons, green beans and potatoes, and now my dream is to have a veggie patch. (Remember: I'm the person who never used to eat vegetables . . .)

I just feel SO much better. I used to get really bad stomach problems when I ate nothing but bread – and as soon as I stopped that I've had no problems with my belly. AT ALL. I've had no acid reflux, no bloat, nothing like that.

I actually still weigh the same, but eating differently has helped my body keep in shape and helped my mood, too.

*I might not look different to you (and that's not the point I'm making) but I feel different.*

I feel less tired and more motivated. I used to have no energy to do anything.

ALL BECAUSE OF FOOD.

It's crazy, isn't it? But it's true.

So, all I wanna say is *please* think about what you're putting into your bodies. They are precious. Forget what anyone else says about THIS DIET and THAT MIRACULOUS PILL – that's bollocks. Veggie life might not be for you, those random diets might not be for you, but find something that keeps your body healthy. Your body is unique – so do what suits YOU.

# IF YOU'RE FEELING S**T ABOUT YOURSELF . . . START GIVING COMPLIMENTS

For so long I felt bad and didn't think I was pretty and didn't like my body. In fact, I used to feel angry at beautiful people because I felt ugly. So, if anyone complimented me, I wouldn't believe them. *Because I didn't feel like that about myself.*

*People may have said nice things to me but I always thought they were lying.*

There was no way I could think that thing about myself, so they MUST have been lying, right?

Wrong.

It's really important for you to know: as soon as I started liking myself, I was more able to take a compliment (and even a negative comment for that matter). If someone says something nice about my face, my hair, my outfit – whatever it is, I'm better now at being able to say 'Thanks!' I do sometimes find it hard to accept that people are telling the truth (being real with you, I still do have massive trust issues) but I'm getting better. I know now that most people are being genuine and nice. And I've learned to admire someone else's beauty without questioning my own.

There is a good reason why we find it difficult to remember compliments but can easily hold on to criticisms – it's called the negativity bias. Basically, psychologists have proved that humans remember negative experiences more strongly than positive ones (they're even processed in totally different parts of our brains!) So it's not our fault that we tend to pick up on the nasty stuff, and remember it, rather than the times when people say nice things about us.

But we can help each other feel better. We can compliment each other and boost each other's self-esteem, 'cause when we make someone else feel good it makes us feel good too. Win win.

So, compliment someone. Don't comment on someone's weight, but think of something else positive you can say to them. If you like someone's outfit, TELL THEM. If you like their hair, TELL THEM. If you like their shoes, TELL THEM. If you like their smile, TELL THEM.

If you think something nice about someone else, just bloody well tell them. It could make their day. Or their week. Imagine that.

**Here's the three nicest compliments I've ever received**
1. 'You're a really good songwriter'
2. 'You have an amazingly positive and lovely energy'
3. 'That's a perfect cuppa!'

# THE THREE NICEST COMPLIMENTS YOU'VE EVER RECEIVED

*1*
........................................................................
........................................................................
*2*
........................................................................
........................................................................
*3*
........................................................................
........................................................................
........................................................................

# THREE NICE COMPLIMENTS YOU CAN SEND YOUR FRIENDS TODAY

*1*
........................................................................
........................................................................
*2*
........................................................................
........................................................................
*3*
........................................................................
........................................................................

## A love-letter to my body – and yours

My body has loved me since the day I was born. Even when I was horrible to it, it kept me going. It's time to take care of it. Me and my body are a team. We are going to live this life together. I will treat it with the utmost respect and say thank you, for keeping me alive. I thank you, my brain, for how much you go through and still try to make everything make sense. You are one in 7.9 billion in the world. You are a one-off and you are mine. I will celebrate my differences and care for you like you've cared for me since I took my first breath.

*This is your reminder that you are more than your appearance.*

Love your eyebrows. Love your nose. Love your lips. Love your ears. Love your chin. Love your cheeks. Love your eyes. Love your soul. Because YOU ARE BEAUTIFUL. Stop worrying about people looking at you. They are not worried about your body or your face, they are thinking about what their body and face looks like. And stop tryna look like someone else. You are the ONLY one with your face – isn't that incredible? Work with what you have. Accept your beauty.

Beauty = being different and being different = perfection.

And while we're at it – let's get rid of this idea that you need to be 'perfect'. Apparently, the dictionary says it's: complete and correct in every way, without fault.

Let's redefine that. Because it's impossible to be a 'perfect person'. No one is without fault. No one is correct in every way. We are all full of bumps and lumps and cracks and mistakes – and that's exactly as it should be. We're all perfectly imperfect, and that's what makes us unique and AMAZING.

You are perfectly imperfect just the way you are.

(And if you're still not feeling great, I always find dancing around my living room gets me in a good mood . . .)

As long as I have
found myself / To win
sometimes you lose

# Mental health, self-care and how therapy saved me

**W**hen I was probably at the lowest I've ever felt, I read a book called *Reasons to Stay Alive,* by Matt Haig. He's an author who's written lots of books, but this one is about his own journey with depression. It's a really incredible book, and the overall message is that you can change the way you feel, rather than looking for change. It's totally about Matt's life but it feels like a guidebook that anyone can use to help them if they're struggling – which I was.

When I read books, I highlight the sentences and words that stick out most to me – the ones I relate to the most. I dunno why. I just like it.

I'm in a different place now than when I marked up this book. But recently I was intrigued to see what spoke to me at the time. So, I re-opened the book. It wasn't nice. And it brought back a lot of pain. On the next page is what I had highlighted.

I got out of that place, even though I didn't think I'd be able to. But I did, and I'm here. Therapy, and being able to really explore my feelings, has totally changed my life, but it's been a proper rocky road.

*I can remember the day*

*the old me dies.*

*Some biological activity in*

*the rear of my skull.*

*I just thought I was about to die.*

*And then I started to go.*

## From popular girl to social outcast

It's so weird to think that I went from being the funny, loud, confident kid without a care in the world, to someone who was filled with anxiety about every single aspect to their life. Someone who thought that everyone was out to get her, who was obsessive and terrified to be honest about her emotions.

But that's what happened.

I know exactly when things started to go bad for me. It was an incident at secondary school that turned me from a popular girl with lots of friends to a total outcast: someone who was embarrassed that they had no friends and began to hold all that shame inside. The after-effects of this time affected my mental health for so many years.

And do you know what's really mad? It's that looking back at what I did now, I realise it's such a tiny, nothing thing. It's ridiculous really, but this was the incident that turned everyone against me.

OK, so let's set the scene. At secondary school, I'd been doing all right, as I said. I was part of the 'main' popular group of girls at school, and had boyfriends. This was at the time where you'd literally swap boyfriends each day in the playground – going up to people and saying, 'You're dumped, I'm going out with him now.'

At thirteen years old, when I was in Year 9, I was going out with one of the popular boys, we'll call him Jamie. One night I phoned one of his friends, Reece, and spoke to him. That was all it was – *I spoke to him on the phone*. Admittedly, it was in a flirty way, I remember I fancied him (to be honest *everyone* fancied everyone at that point) but I didn't actually *do* anything.

The phone call itself though was enough. Word got out really quickly that I'd spoken to Reece, and my boyfriend Jamie suddenly hated me. Not only that, but overnight, it felt like everyone at school also turned against me because Jamie was the cousin of the most popular boy in school; and the popular people in our school had control over who was in, and who was out. I had been part of that crowd, and suddenly, I wasn't. People stopped speaking to me, they wouldn't sit next to me in lessons – they would blank me. I couldn't walk down the corridor without people saying something nasty to me, or threatening that they'd meet me in the toilets to do me over.

I had nowhere I could feel comfortable or safe. The atmosphere in school was honestly like I had killed someone – people were treating me like I was a murderer. The annoying thing was, Reece was absolutely fine, no one hated him. Even Jamie stayed friends with him. What the f**k?!

## Being too ashamed to tell anyone

Obviously, this all made me feel so sad. I blamed myself. I had cheated –
well, at least that's what I felt I'd done. I cast myself as a terrible person, and
started to feel properly unhappy deep inside. That was when I changed.

*I shut down emotionally, as my way
of coping with the situation.*

I went mute at school – I didn't want to say anything in case people
would pick up on it and hate me even more.

What made it much worse was that I didn't tell anyone at home what
was going on. They had no idea. They thought I was still really happy,
outgoing and had loads of friends. I thought it was best to let them keep
thinking that.

This was a big mistake, though. If I had just gone home to my mum and
dad and said, 'Look, this is happening at school,' they would have helped
me. They could have just said one sentence that would have made me
feel loads better, and been able to put it all into perspective. But I was
too ashamed about what I'd 'done' and so I felt completely stuck. I let my
problems get worse and worse.

## Acting out my unhappiness

About a year after the incident, a boy confronted me at school. He'd known
me since I was tiny, and obviously was confused about why I was letting
everyone pick on me like that (not that *he* was being any nicer, but still).
'Why do you never stand up for yourself?' he asked me. I sat there all

lesson long, asking myself that question.

From that moment on, my behaviour changed — it was like something inside me switched.

> I decided I didn't want to be the victim anymore and so instead I became an angry, horrible person to the people I loved most.

Honestly, I was a proper bitch. I was naughty and rude to the teachers at school, and really, really hateful towards my parents. They thought I was just going through typical teenage behaviour — they had no idea all my negative energy was coming from school because I still hadn't told them. I was so nasty to them, it was awful. I still apologise to this day to my parents for what I was like to them back then.

My mum and dad thought I was just being a little pr*ck, but safe in my bedroom, I'd cry a lot. The torment went on for so long — even up to when I did my GCSEs. I remember having to run from my exams to the train station, so no one would know that I had left, otherwise they'd run after me.

At one point I got so sad, I sat in my room and texted a couple of my friends. Well, they were girls who'd been my friends previously, but ever since the incident with Jamie and Reece, they'd cut me off. I was so miserable and lonely, I sent them a message saying I wanted to die. It was a cry for help. I don't think I ever thought about dying, I just wanted them to know how sad I felt. It was a living nightmare, to be honest.

I didn't tell my parents, or anyone, about this for years afterwards. I should have done. Because it did so much damage to my mental health, and to my life, for a long time.

# IF YOU'RE EVER FEELING AS BAD AS THIS . . .

I know that things can often seem desperate – you can be in a place where you honestly feel like things can never get any better. But they can. I promise you that.

    If you're ever feeling this fragile and low, you HAVE to call someone – anyone. Just tell somebody how you're feeling, and they will be able to help.

    Never give up. You might feel like you're stuck now, but things will get better. Your life is worth living.

    Some places to find help if you need it:

> You can contact Samaritans 24 hours a day, 365 days a year. You can call 116 123 (free from any phone) or email jo@samaritans.org

> SANEline. If you're experiencing a mental health problem or supporting someone else, you can call SANEline on 0300 304 7000 (4.30 p.m.–10.30 p.m. every day)

> Visit the MIND website for help https://www.mind.org.uk

> The Mix. If you're under 25, you can call The Mix on 0808 808 4994, or email them here: https://www.themix.org.uk/get-support/speak-to-our-team/email-us

## Fake friends and losing trust

While I was being mugged off by the 'popular' kids, other people at school started to behave differently towards me too. A few different people – the ones who were more the outcasts themselves – would talk to me, because I guess they knew how it felt. This confused me, because growing up in that kinda school you learned from your friends that cool kids were the best people and 'geeks' were uncool and weird. But making friends with them in Year 10 changed that whole skewed judgement. While I still pretended with these new friends that I was OK, and would say to them, 'I'm fine, I don't care,' about everything, even when it wasn't true, they made school bearable for me. I'm really grateful they reached out to me at that time.

A few of the girls I used to be friends with also felt bad about what I was going through. These were the girls who I'd texted when I told them I wanted to die. Outside of school they'd message and call me sometimes, asking if I was OK. But they'd never do that in front of other people. When we were in school, the same girls who'd been telling me not to worry would completely blank me.

It really baffled me. I couldn't work out why people would be nice to me one moment, and s\*\*t to me the next. These 'secret friendships' (that actually weren't friendships AT ALL, let's be honest) really f\*\*ked me up.

*I started to develop trust issues, because I realised that their niceness was fake.*

It wasn't real. It rocked my view of the world, and I began thinking that people weren't good. That everyone was putting on a false front and that everyone was lying.

That idea that nothing was what it seemed, that people couldn't be trusted became a huge issue for me. And I took that into adulthood.

## WHAT I WISH I'D KNOWN BACK THEN:

> Everyone is going through a tricky time in their teenage years — I was just a convenient punching bag

> Even the people who seem most confident on the outside really aren't on the inside

> You'll make real friends soon — these people won't matter at all to you in a few years' time

> School is NOT the be-all and end-all of your life!

> Being an arsey cow to everyone isn't a great way of dealing with your problems . . .

> Just open your mouth and be HONEST — telling someone how you feel and what's happening will make all the difference

> DO NOT be embarrassed about the mistakes you've made.

## My mental health gets worse

When you're at school, nearly everyone wants to be popular. So when you're not – when you're that person who is really hated, like I felt I was – it messes with you. It feels like the worst thing ever, and because I wasn't liked I went to the other extreme of desperately *wanting* to be liked. And it got worse even as I got into my twenties – I'd go out and meet new people and all I could think was, *I really want you to like me,* and start stressing that they didn't.

It became a bigger and bigger problem, which got more complicated by my trust issues. I genuinely believed that people were evil. My approach was that you couldn't be too careful, because something bad was always round the corner. For example, I'd be really aware that murderers look normal, like ordinary people walking around. So I convinced myself that *I* would be the person to catch them out, which meant I'd be constantly looking around, sussing people out, assuming they were about to do something bad. I thought I was a f**king hawk eye, and that it was down to me to protect others.

I'd always had that over-protective streak. I remember one occasion from when I was twelve and went out shopping with my sister. A man looked at her for a bit too long and I immediately fronted up to him, saying, 'What the f**k are you looking at?' Of course, this can be a really dangerous way to behave, but my over-protectiveness was made even worse when paired with my paranoia that people were out to get me, that they always had bad intentions. I was constantly focused on what people said, what they did, what they touched, trying to 'catch' them out. But it was such a stressful place to be in, on constant high alert. I can see that now.

It's clear how confusing this is, right? That on the one hand I was desperate for people to like me, but on the other, I thought those same people were evil and untrustworthy? How the hell do those things work together? Well, they don't. They mess you up inside.

Because I thought there was danger everywhere, I was constantly worried about bad things happening. My therapist says I have OCD tendencies and this is definitely where they started to kick in. If my family or good friends were at their own houses, I couldn't know when they were leaving – because if I did, I would feel really strongly that something bad would happen to them.

It was such a damaging thing, this belief that I could control their outcomes. I'd get weird little random thoughts like that all the time – ones like, *Oh, if you don't move this bottle of water to* that *position, your family are gonna die.* It felt like I had special psychic powers, and the universe was giving me some kind of warning so that I could control and protect people this way.

## My emotions spiral downwards

As I got more well known, in my mid-twenties, this got harder. More people looking at me, more people to figure out. I'd really struggle because as soon as someone looked at me I thought they'd hate me. Yes, I know – I was the person who thought everyone was evil. But I was constantly worried that they'd think I was a bad person, too. I didn't trust people, but I didn't trust myself, either.

Things got worse and worse. I eventually found it incredibly difficult just to get out of my car and walk somewhere from fear of people looking at me. I stopped answering the door and the phone when it rang. I was on constant high alert worrying that evil people would cause harm to my family and I would have panic attacks in the night where I felt like half my brain was here, and the other part was halfway to dying – episodes of disassociation. (Disassocation is a type of mental health problem where you feel disconnected from your body and the world around you – although it can be different for everyone). I'd google 'psychosis', where you perceive or interpret reality in a different way from people around you, because I was convinced that was what was happening to me.

I didn't have any balance in my life. All my emotions were either extremely happy or extremely sad. I couldn't find the middle ground. On the surface, I had success – my music career had taken off, I had good people around me, I was doing well – but inside, I felt completely differently. In my head, I was unsuccessful, my music career was failing and everyone around me was gonna mug me off. Stressful, huh?

## When I realised what sad really meant

One day, in the thick of all this, at one of my lowest points,

*I realised that feeling sad didn't just mean crying.*

I was so sad that I *couldn't* cry.

It was a deeper feeling than that. A new meaning. A meaning for sad that I wish I never figured out or felt. But I did. I went to a cognitive behavioural therapist (CBT) for the first time in my life. She told me that I was on the verge of a full-on breakdown, and that I was severely depressed.

I was still promoting my first album *Speak Your Mind* and recording some new material at this time, but to help myself, I stopped working for a bit. I pulled recording sessions and stayed at home. I saw the CBT therapist for two sessions, but then didn't see the point of it anymore. Staying at home also didn't make anything better. I was stuck in the same place, mentally and emotionally, and like at school, toyed with the idea of not being here anymore. It crossed my mind a lot. I never thought, *Would my family and friends miss me?* or *Do they care about me?*, It was always *I don't want to feel this anymore*. It was only about my feelings, and I didn't wanna feel those feelings anymore.

Depression is selfish. I didn't find anything fun anymore. I was trying to feel fun, doing things I used to do, going to the cinema, bowling, karaoke, but nothing would work.

*I was stuck with no emotion. I wasn't sad, or happy. I was numb. I'd hit rock bottom.*

The only thing that I knew at that point, though, was that it couldn't get any worse. It could only get better. That was my hope and that's what I held on to.

The day I realised that, I started to write down lists of what I needed to try to make me feel better. Here's the first few things from the list I wrote then:

1: Therapy
2: Sleep doctor
3: Work out
4: Food
5: Remove negative energy/people

Also, every evening, I started to write down the bad and good things that had happened that day, and my goals for the next day.

Things like that started to help me piece myself back together. But it wasn't until I found the right therapist to really work through all my problems that I turned a corner and transformed my life for the better.

# BOOK CLUB WITH ANNE-MARIE!

These books have helped me with my mental health so much, and I've learned a lot from them:

*Notes on a Nervous Planet* by Matt Haig: this really helped me understand why most of us feel anxious in the modern world. It's a great book about the effects of technology on our brains, and how we deal with it. After reading it I started to come off my phone a bit more! Matt's writing style is really conversational and easy to follow. It's the perfect book to dip in and out of if you don't want to read in long stretches.

*The Subtle Art of Not Giving a F**k* by Mark Manson: when I first read this book, it became my favourite thing ever. It's SO good. The message in this is that you should learn what is most important to care about and ditch what isn't. I used to care about literally every tiny little thing (like what people thought of me), and this has helped me put things into perspective. He has a really direct, opinionated writing voice too, which I love.

*Why We Sleep: Unlocking the Power of Sleep and Dreams* by Matthew Walker: this is a much deeper read, as it goes into all the scientific evidence about why sleep is so vital. If you're fed up with people just saying, 'oh you need to sleep otherwise you'll feel crap', then this book is the one to help you. It goes into real depth about how sleep helps our brains in all types of different ways – I found it fascinating.

> *The Boy, the Mole, the Fox and the Horse* by Charlie Mackesy: the first time I read this book it made me cry, actually every time I read this book I cry – it's so beautiful. I read this whenever I feel like s\*\*t, as it's so lovely and uplifting. It's a story about a boy meeting these animals and learning things along the way, and essentially the message is all about being a kind and decent human. I've bought this book so many times and given it as gifts to my friends.

## Starting therapy, and finding answers

My manager Jazz has been there for me for years, and has always been brilliant at helping me find my way through. A few years after trying CBT, I was still unhappy and she could see that I needed help and that my way of thinking – that it was everything and everyone *else* who was against me – was making me sad. She was the one who proposed I try therapy the first time around and while it hadn't worked so well, because I didn't connect with the therapist, she brought it up again, suggesting now might be the perfect time to give it another go and find someone new.

She introduced me to my therapist, we'll call her C, and during our first session, I just poured my heart out. The difference was that this time, rather than just listening to me, she asked questions. She started digging around inside my brain, questioning why I thought certain things, and really starting to break down the assumptions I'd had for years. The belief systems that I was convinced were right and true.

I'm fascinated with how the brain works, and she started to help me understand what was going on underneath my immediate feelings. Working with C has unravelled every single little thought from the surface

layer and connected it all together. Like puzzle pieces. It's been incredible.
I can say without any doubt that

*when I started to understand what's happening in my brain, that's when things started to change for the better.*

Going to therapy once a week – which I still do – has changed my life.
The beauty of talking and letting things out never fails us. I don't know if I'd
be here without it. And if I was, I would still be the same person as before.
Which was impossible.

# IF YOU'RE FEELING SAD . . .
# WAYS TO LET IT ALL OUT

I know not everyone can access a therapist easily. But there are loads of other ways you can help yourself when you're feeling rubbish. First of all, being aware of how you're feeling is the first step. Don't compare your problems negatively with others. Your problem is NEVER too small to do something about it.

### Writing:

When I feel crap, I write things down. I've learned that putting my thoughts and feelings down on paper (or even a phone screen), however weird it feels at the beginning, is incredible at helping me cope with my emotions.

### Talking:

It is so good to talk to absolutely anyone about how you're feeling – even if you're not sure how to describe it straight off. Just start a casual conversation with anyone you trust – a friend, a parent, a colleague. It doesn't have to be scary. You don't need to know everything or understand everything you are feeling to start a chat about it.

### Ted Talks & Youtube Videos:

One of the things I find most helpful when I feel like s**t is to look up Ted Talks about that emotion. I've watched so many incredible talks and videos where experts have been able to explain how I'm feeling better than I can! It's amazing, it helps me feel like I'm not the only one experiencing my emotions and I learn so much, too.

With all this, I've discovered how good it is to be curious. Be curious about your feelings, even if you can't really work out what they are straight away, or don't have the words to articulate it with someone. Whether it's something you're feeling in your belly, your body, or your head, there are so many incredible resources out there that have different answers. Be inquisitive about your brain.

## My 'Wonky Beliefs' and how therapy helped me understand them

The result of all the therapy I've had is amazing. C has really helped me with my brain, by explaining to me what was really going on, deep down. Even if you can't access a therapist, and I know not everyone can, try to think about what your wonky beliefs are – things that aren't really true. (Of course, I'm not saying you should rely on Dr Google to self-diagnose. If you think you have a serious problem, you should always seek professional help). Here are mine:

### My wonky belief that people were evil

As mentioned earlier, I had such an obsession with this. I used to think, *Oh my god, maybe I should be a detective, I have some sort of psychic powers*. My therapist was like, 'No, you're not. You're hyper-aware, you're hyper-vigilant.' I was like, *Oh*, I googled it, and yeah, she was right.

She named it for me. And doing that really put things into context. It helped me realise I'm not some sort of one-off extreme person having these thoughts. It's actually my brain just working in a state of hyper-vigilance. Knowing this has made me happier and taken a massive load off my shoulders (or inside my head!)

### My wonky belief I could control the future

I was convinced that my OCD tendencies were protecting my family from something awful happening to them. But my therapist questioned that. She asked me outright, 'Why do you think you can control someone's death?' I was like, 'Well, because something's telling me!' It started a conversation about death. We soon realised I have a fear of it and from there we figured out where it all comes from and why I thought I could control people's outcomes.

Working jointly, we were able to piece together where this all started from and why I was so worried about horrible things happening. It's because my sister Sam nearly died when I was fourteen. She suddenly came down with meningitis. We didn't know it straight away: she just developed this rash on her belly and started to feel really ill. That night, she started vomiting, but didn't say anything to my parents because she didn't want to worry them. The next morning, she rolled out of bed, unconscious. We called the ambulance, and the paramedic gave her an antibiotic shot, which we found out later saved her life.

It was completely terrifying, but after she got back home from hospital and recovered, we never talked about it again as a family. (Which isn't right, by the way!)

I used to feel these thoughts were an outer energy from the universe telling me that something bad was going to happen. But my therapist helped me realise that it's not that, it's not some mysterious power. It's not about me being psychic and having a hawk eye (shame). It's just my worries and stresses, and my not wanting people to die, because I've seen how scarily quick it could happen. These beliefs were my way of trying to control those fears, which of course doesn't actually work.

It's so good to know what it was. I know I'll never stop having those thoughts entirely, but I am having way fewer of those moments.

### My wonky belief that I couldn't trust anyone

Having those huge trust issues made me paranoid that when people did stuff wrong, it was because they wanted to mug me off. So for example, someone I used to work with ages ago always messed things up a bit. I used to think, *Rah, he just wants me to be s\*\*t, he wants me to fail, he hates me,* but my therapist was like, 'Um, no. Maybe he's just bad at his job?' I was like, *OH!* (She was right about that, too).

Understanding this has been SO good. That it's not all about me, that most of the time, people aren't thinking about doing me dirty, they're just living their own life.

To be honest, I'm still processing my issues, but I understand now that not trusting people is only damaging to your own energy. If you go through your everyday life thinking everyone is a bad person, then it's totally draining. It turns you angry and cynical. Believing that people are good until proven otherwise is a way better way of living. And I'm still working on that.

### My wonky belief that I had to be liked, by everyone

Worrying about what other people might be thinking about you is so exhausting. Working with my therapist helped me see that I can't control this. I can't make everyone like me. And it's 100 per cent certain that not everyone will. But that's OK. And why would I want everyone to like me? I mean – *I* don't like everyone. Why do I expect everyone to like me?

As soon as I realised this, I became happier. Not to say I didn't have happy moments before, but everything was influenced by worrying what others think.

# A QUICK EXERCISE TO LET GO OF WORRY AND BE YOURSELF

OK, so here's an easy little exercise you can do anywhere, at any time, to help you let go of worry when you're feeling overwhelmed.

Firstly, find somewhere comfortable to sit.

Take a deep breath.

Just for five minutes imagine yourself without worrying what everyone thinks about you. Just walking around, thinking your own thoughts – not what others are thinking about you.

Close your eyes and imagine you, without the worry.

It is SO freeing. Doing stuff 'cause you want to. Wearing whatever you want to.

Open your eyes.

Now you've imagined it, you can actually do it . . . try it! Become that person you just imagined.

It takes practice, but trust me. It works.

*Every day I let go of worry a little more. And it feels so good.*

Because if you're constantly worrying about what other people are thinking, you'll never be your true self. Think about it – you'll be constantly changing little bits of yourself to fit in and adjust their opinions of you.

Life really is too short to live through other people's optics. It's all in your own imagination, anyway. So what's the point in worrying? And WHO CARES? Your life is yours.

When you let go of that worry your life gets way more fun, too! You become your true self. Just you. You don't even have to try, because it's just who you are. When you're comfortable and in love with yourself, you won't really care if everyone likes you or not. Because YOU like YOU. And YOU will be happy.

# MY LIST OF RANDOM STUFF THAT MAKES ME FEEL BETTER:

Snow | Sun | Talking to my plants | Big hats | Backpacks | Vegetables | Books | Yoga | Bingo | *Judge Judy* | Cuddles | *Say Yes to the Dress* | Lego | Jigsaws | The smell of rain | Candles

# YOUR LIST OF RANDOM STUFF THAT MAKES YOU FEEL BETTER

........................................................................................................

........................................................................................................

........................................................................................................

........................................................................................................

........................................................................................................

........................................................................................................

........................................................................................................

........................................................................................................

........................................................................................................

## My biggest revelations from therapy

*Confronting all my issues has transformed my life.*

And it's all down to working out with my therapist *why* I feel how I do. It's that digging deeper, looking beneath the surface, naming my feelings and understanding how my brain is working when these things happen. It's about understanding that it's not just me being a weirdo!

Speaking about my feelings, and being able to explain them, is incredible. Going through this process has made me wanna tell everyone about it. And it's also helped me open up to people I never did before. I actually sat down with my mum and dad recently to tell them about what happened at school. All the stuff I never shared with them at the time.

They were both shocked. My dad even said he wouldn't have been so hard on me at home if he'd known what I was going through. I was being a d*ck at home, like I said, and they were punishing me for being like that, so I'd be sad, locked away in my room. 'If only we'd known, we could have made this a safe place for you,' my dad said. It made me wish I'd told them before, but you can't change the past.

It was an amazing conversation to have, though, with them. From that chat about the school situation, they started opening up to me about other stuff, too – something they hadn't done before. In this way, working on myself meant that I was able to make my relationship with my parents better, too. And it's the same for everyone: when you understand yourself better, you can communicate better with the people you love, too, strengthening those foundations.

# IF YOU'RE FEELING SHAME . . . USE THIS

Shame and embarrassment were 100 per cent behind so many of my problems.

I just don't care so much what people think anymore. I'm not going to let that stop me. And I don't want you to, either.

So, if you're feeling in the pit right now, but think that your feelings aren't valid, or aren't important enough, I want you to tell yourself one really important thing:

**MY FEELINGS ARE NEVER SHAMEFUL**

Say it. Inside your head and out loud right now – five times at least. Go on, do it! Also, repeat it every time you doubt yourself. Use it as an affirmation.

I first learned about the power of affirmations when my OCD tendencies were getting really bad. They're short, positive statements that you repeat in order to challenge negative or self-sabotaging thoughts. I discovered that saying a mantra over and over again could make me feel better. By repeating the same phrase, you start to believe every word of that sentence. It works. Try it! (This is the one I use: my family, my friends and I will live long enough to become who we are meant to be.)

## A few words on . . . WALKING and why I love it

I used to think walking was really boring. In fact, I used to HATE it. I couldn't see the point. Whenever I'd go for a walk – which was very rare – it would always be because someone else forced me to go. This wasn't because I didn't like being around nature – in fact, I've always had a love for spending time around trees and greenery (I even bought the place I live in because it has an amazing view of a tree from the living-room window!). But walking? Forget it.

I don't know what it was, but one day I thought to myself: *I'm going to go for a walk in the forest.* I suddenly had this urge to be with nature, on my own.

*I spent two hours walking around and I can honestly say it was the best two hours of my life.*

I'd listen to the leaves and twigs cracking under my feet, I sat on a big tree trunk and let my mind wander. It started to rain, and so I sheltered under a tree canopy and watched the rain come down through the clouds. People were walking by and I didn't care what they thought. It just felt like heaven to me.

Whenever I had gone for walks before, I'd do something to distract myself – whether that was being on my phone, listening to music or chatting to someone I was with. But when I was on my own, I was in the moment. It was that awareness of being present that made me feel so calm and happy.

So, go for a walk if you can. Make sure it's somewhere safe – that's the most important thing. And when you do, give yourself those moments where you disconnect from everything (yes, EVEN YOUR PHONE) and just exist in the world.

The Swedish call those moments of slowing down and appreciating the good things in life *fika*. It's a really important part of their country's culture. I found my *fika* when I went for that incredible walk. See if you can too.

# MY FEEL-BETTER PLAYLIST

If you're not ready to try going for a walk completely without distraction, then here's a playlist of the songs that always make me feel better when I wake up in a mood. Maybe create a playlist of your own to listen to on your walks as you work towards walking alone.

Christina Aguilera – 'Soar'

HONNE – 'Warm on a Cold Night'

José González – 'Heartbeats'

John Mayer – '3x5'

Kendrick Lamar – 'DNA'

MGMT – 'Electric Feel'

Omar – 'Golden Brown'

Oren Lavie – 'Her Morning Elegance'

Sia – 'Beautiful Calm Driving'

Stormzy – 'Superheroes'

Shakka – 'Strength of an Ox'

Toots and the Maytals – '54-46 Was My Number'

Vampire Weekend – 'Harmony Hall'

## A few words on . . . SLEEPING and why I used to hate it

I've always had problems with sleep. When I was at school I'd just not be tired at night-time – I had too much energy! I'd honestly be up until 4 a.m. some nights, and then wake up at 7 a.m. to go to school. I knew I was 'supposed' to sleep more, because everyone was telling me to. I wasn't being disobedient and difficult on purpose, I just found sleep pointless and boring and I just wasn't tired.

The older I got, the worse my issues with sleep got – especially when I started touring. I'd get home from a gig, and into my hotel room, which would be one room with a bed in it. I'd feel so much pressure from that, like YOU HAVE TO GO TO SLEEP NOW, and it got so bad, I stopped being able to sleep on a bed! I hated bedrooms in general, and that really fed into my insomnia.

I even went to see a sleep doctor at one point: but he just gave me sleeping pills, which made me feel groggy in the morning. I stopped taking them, but then found I couldn't sleep AT ALL without them, so I went onto Night Nurse and Day Nurse, which was another problem in and of itself. Deep down, I still hated the idea of sleeping, and medication hadn't helped me address my anxieties about night-time.

It wasn't until I read the book *Why We Sleep* that things started to fall into place for me. In it, I learned that there are so many important physical and physiological benefits behind sleeping, one of which is to allow our brains to store memories. (I had a massive problem with remembering things, which was probably because of my sleep issues.)

I also learned about the idea of body clocks, and the fact that some people, like me, naturally have longer body clocks than others. We're all brought up to believe we should fall asleep at 10 p.m. and wake up at 7 a.m., but not all of us are built like that! Some of us can stay awake longer.

*Society is built around a clock
that doesn't suit everyone,
least of all me.*

Knowing that has really helped me – as well as only going into my bedroom when I'm actually tired. My relationship with sleep is still a work in progress, but I think it's important not to put yourself under pressure if you're not a great sleeper. We've all got different body clocks – some of us are early birds and some of us are night owls – and getting stressed if you don't fit into the rigid timetable is only gonna make things worse.

## Why I don't regret the past

Sometimes I look back and wish I hadn't gone through all those s**t times – they made me unhappy for so long and took away from a lot of the exciting things I've experienced.

But then I remember what I've learned from them. That negative emotions can be good and are good to feel – because it's from there that you grow and change. The worst moment of my life was also the most transitional. From pain comes beauty.

## JOKES FOR WHEN NOTHING ELSE WORKS AND YOU NEED SOMETHING TO MAKE YOU SMILE

You know what? Sometimes I'm just having a s**t day, and nothing makes me feel better – not a playlist, not walking, not anything. I'm still in a massive mood. If this is where you're finding yourself, then it's definitely time for the cheesy jokes.

What do you call a Frenchman wearing sandals?
*Phillipe Phloppe.*

Why are dumb-blonde jokes so short?
*So men can remember them.*

My girlfriend and I often laugh about how competitive we are.
*But I laugh more.*

Two fish are in a tank. One turns to the other and says,
*'Hey, do you know how to drive this thing?'*

Coz that's just who I am / If you don't like it don't give a damn / Got enough drama I don't need fake friends

# Learning what real friendship is all about

**W**hen I was at college, studying BTEC performing arts, we did a group exercise called a 'Truth Circle'. This was a few months into the course, so we'd all got to know each other a little bit by then. The idea behind it was that everyone had to be totally honest about our first impressions of each other.

Everyone's first impressions of me? That I was a bitch. I guess I'd given off a real 'don't come near me' energy, as if I didn't want to talk to anyone. Everyone had thought I was really off with them, and that I wasn't interested at all in making friends.

I felt sad when I heard this, and apologised – I didn't ever want anyone to think I was a horrible person. And it was the COMPLETE opposite of how I wanted to come across.

But I knew why they had that impression. Because of what I'd been through at school, I carried that same attitude with me – believing that nobody would like me and I couldn't trust anyone. So, at college, that obviously influenced how I came across.

*I was defensive and hard on the outside, but inside I was just a muddle of anxiety.*

This made it really difficult for me to open myself up to people and make friends properly.

*FRIENDSHIP TRUTH #1:*
*don't let others' opinions of you*
*be your opinion of yourself*

## Still having a warped perception

My idea of what friendship was like was still completely skewed when I was in performing arts college. My experience at school of being frozen out and tormented by those people who I thought were my friends meant I was still shut down emotionally.

I was still so desperate to be liked, but I thought the reason I didn't have any proper friends was my own fault. *These people don't like me because I'm a terrible person* was the mantra that would loop around inside my head. It was painful, and I had that same mindset when I started college – even though I did go on to meet some good friends.

I've been doing so much thinking in the past few years about this time. Now, looking back, I've realised:

*I wouldn't be the person I am today if I hadn't gone through what I did.*

I wouldn't be such a deep thinker, I wouldn't be as aware of everything around me, and as empathetic to others. Now, I'm thankful for that time. It doesn't stop it from being total crap, though!

## IF YOU'RE FEELING LONELY . . . THESE ARE SOME TRUTHS

I know what it's like to feel lonely. As if no one likes you, that you're the most unpopular person alive, and like there's something wrong with you deep down that stops people liking you. It's a horrible emotion, I know! But it will be OK. I promise.

### Feelings aren't facts

First of all, you've gotta remember that if you're feeling like this, it doesn't mean it's true. There isn't anything wrong with you. If some people don't like you, it doesn't matter! You're alive, you're OK and you know you have good intentions – so who cares? It's their loss.

### Give it time

Sometimes it takes a long time to find your tribe, to meet and connect with the people that really 'get' you. You can't expect it to all fall into place straight away, so don't stress about it. One day, you'll find like-minded people and you have your WHOLE life to do it in.

### Solitude vs loneliness

Remember, too: you are your own friend, so you already have the best friend possible. And there's a huge amount to be said for the joy of solitude – where you choose to spend time alone – which is very different to loneliness.

I've taught myself how to love solitude in recent years. I used to be the sort of person who *had* to have someone around me all the time – I thought I couldn't function without someone with me, and I even used to go and sit on train platforms just so I could have people walking past! But I had to face being on my own – I really wanted to be able to go for a walk on my own. So I forced myself to do it. The first time I did it I hated it, I felt weird and crazy, but I pushed myself through it and tried a few more times. Just like anything, over time you start to enjoy it (just like eating an olive!)
Now I love being on my own, and it's such a relaxing place to be in.

## Starting to make new friends

When I started college, there were loads of people there who'd gone to my school. This absolutely terrified me, as I felt trapped by the reputation I'd had back then. I was so scared the school people would tell the new college people that I was a d*ck, I wanted to remove myself from anyone who knew me. I wanted to separate my old life from my new, so I started hanging around with a totally new crowd. They messed about a lot, though, and I started to slack off massively – which went on to cause me big problems later on.

Doing my course did have an upside, though, as I did start to make some actual friends – especially my friend Nikk. Initially, I was a bit freaked out upon meeting her, because she knew the same people I did from back at school. But we were so similar and got on straight away. It was really nice to have a real friend, someone I felt liked me for who I was, no matter what had gone on at school.

## Finding out what true friendship meant

After college, I started doing local talent shows. My dad would take me along each weekend, where I'd sing all around Essex, mainly in pubs. It was then, aged eighteen, that I met the person who would become one of the most important people in my life – but the way we met was quite hilarious (and very me).

Bizarrely, I already knew Claire. We'd both been at the same weekend dance school, but her being older than me, we'd never got properly friendly then. At this point, she'd gone on to become a professional singer and performer, and was actually one of the judges at this talent show. I'd gone on stage to perform, and she recognised me, saying, 'I know you from dance school!' *OK, great,* I thought, and went on to sing my song, 'How Come You Don't Call Me' by Alicia Keys.

After I performed, she leant over to whisper something to one of the other judges. Remember how suspicious I was of everyone, thinking they were out to get me? Well, I saw her do that and I fronted up to her straight away, saying really aggressively, 'What are you saying about me!?' – I automatically thought that she was mugging me off. Claire looked at me, surprised, and replied, 'I was just saying you were really good!'

OH S**T. I got that totally wrong, and nowadays, Claire takes the mick about the way I was then *all the time*. Despite my attitude, we went on to become really good friends. She ran a Motown tribute show, where singers would perform a set featuring famous songs from the sixties, and I got involved too. I spent about three years performing with her act, from eighteen to about twenty. We spent so much time together, and through that, we bonded really tight.

There was so much about Claire that I really admired. Probably because she was that little bit older, she'd been through much more than me – heartbreak, life, moving to another country – whatever it was, she just understood every situation that I was going through, so she always had some good answers. That was amazing to me. Plus, she never ever judged me. Whatever I was going through, she made me feel normal and supported. We became inseparable.

*FRIENDSHIP TRUTH #2:*
*a real friend just wants the best for you*

Claire's helped me through so many s**t times, including that really horrific breakup with Matthew I mentioned before. She knew he was no good for me, and that I wasn't myself with him, so she helped put me back together. I stayed at her house for months while I got over it. I think Claire was the first person who really showed me what friends can do for each other. I'd never had that experience before – friendship felt different with her. We're still close today and I'm godmother to her son.

## Bonding with more good people

As I got more involved with the music industry in my twenties, I got way better at making friends. You're around people all the time: even just gigging, you'll be with a band and a touring crew every day, so there's always about twenty people that you've got to get on with. Even though at this point I still didn't like *myself*, I made a point of being nice to other people.

*Everyone knew me as easy-going, happy, and LOUD!*

It was then that I met someone else who became a really good mate. I've mentioned how I started supporting Rudimental on their tour, and Beanie is their drummer. Just like Claire, he gave me the exact same feeling in my belly – that he was a good person and I was gonna get along really well with him. He's completely genuine and very kind. Once he got to know me, he understood that I got anxious in situations, and would always do his utmost to stick up for me when I needed it. I then met and got friendly with Bridgette, who was also in the band. Just like Beanie and Claire, Bridgette had those similar qualities – she's just a lovely person.

By my mid-twenties I was feeling more confident and happy with the

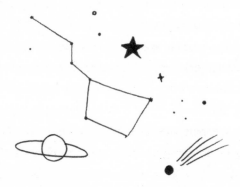

friends I'd made. As with my friend Nikk from college, I felt safer having these individual relationships, rather than being part of a group. If I'd been part of a group, I would worry that they might talk about me behind my back, and persuade other people not to like me. (All that school business was still affecting me.) Herd mentality freaks me out, so I kept it small. And the friends I built up from that time I'm still friends with now.

*FRIENDSHIP TRUTH #3:*
*you don't know what other people are going*
*through, so don't judge so quickly*

## Trusting my gut . . . but moving past first impressions

Gradually, over time, I got way better at becoming friends with people. And with every single one of them, I trusted my gut instinct. I'd feel a pure kindness from them straight away, like a sixth sense or something. That vibe was instant and I'd immediately feel OK about letting my guard down with them. I get that feeling now quite a lot about people – even people on the TV. I look at someone like Stacey Dooley and I'm like, *Oh, she's lovely! I really want to be friends with her!*

Up until recently, I based all my life decisions on believing my gut instincts – not just in friendship. But it hasn't always been the right thing to do, going with your heart 100 per cent rather than thinking things through a bit. I read a really good book called *The Chimp Paradox,* which is all about this: essentially explaining why it's better to be more rational, rather than rely totally on your emotions all the time. Having a balance of the heart *and* head.

Because I've made mistakes this way. Sometimes I've made a rash judgement about someone and thought they were horrible, whereas they're actually lovely (and were just having a bad day). I thought my gut instinct had treated me good, that it had served me well. But I've realised that even though your gut instinct can sometimes be really strong, when it comes to having a *negative* gut instinct, *you can't always rely on the truth of what you're immediately presented with.*

I'll give you an example of a time that really showed me you need to give things a bit longer to make your mind up. I was in my car once at the traffic lights and could see two people nearby. It looked like they were having a proper row – one of them was really shouting at the other one. I got all fired up and was ready to jump out of the car and intervene, but after watching for a moment longer, I realised they *weren't* having a row, it was just that one person was explaining to the other what *someone else had said*. He was telling a story, not being the aggressor. Thank god I stopped myself! I would have run out of the car, all guns blazing, ready to break something up – and been completely wrong. I realised my gut instinct in that instance wasn't right, and it made me question myself on all future gut instincts. I realised I need to take a bit longer to suss out a situation before I make my mind up about people.

*I know that you can get the wrong information about someone from first impressions. I mean – I should know.*

People did it to me at college! I was anxious as f\*\*k and people thought I was a bitch. So, I know now that trusting my gut is one thing, but you've got to give people a little bit more time than just writing them off in those first few moments.

Understanding that you don't know what other people are going through has really changed my mindset. If someone is being a d*ck I know it's because they're going through something else, or they're having a bad day. It's never (or really rarely) about me.

*FRIENDSHIP TRUTH #4:*
*you'll lose friends, you'll fall out with*
*people and that's OK.*

## Situational friendships (and why that's fine)

Another big thing I've learned to accept over the years is that not all friendships last – and THAT'S FINE! I've had friends that I've lost touch with over the years, usually when life circumstances have changed and you don't see them as much anymore. It's not because you hate them, you might have just simply grown apart, the way we do in life. We're not the same people we are when we're seven, twelve, seventeen or twenty-five, so why do we expect our friendships to stay exactly the same throughout everything?

I had a friend I grew apart from a while back, and originally I felt really anxious about it. I didn't want her to feel bad, or think that I was a d*ck. But over time I've come to see it a bit like a relationship ending. When you break up with a partner, people aren't horrified, are they? They don't think *what a terrible person* you are for splitting up! There's an expectation that a relationship will either move to a different level, or you'll end up separating.

*It's fine in relationships to
break up, but for some reason
it's not in friendships.*

There's the idea that once you get a friend you have to stay together for the rest of your life. What's that about?

So I feel OK about things now, because I've come to realise that some friendships are situational. You work with them or you go to school with them, and then when that time comes to an end, maybe you're not destined to carry on as friends past that. And that's OK.

You'll know if you're supposed to stay friends with someone for the long run. You might not be able to see each other all the time anymore, but if you still have that connection with them when you chat, as if time hasn't passed at all, then that's amazing. If friendships are supposed to stick around forever they will.

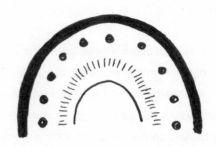

## Breaking up with friends

BUT. Not all friendships *should* last. You don't have to stick with people that make you feel like s**t. You can remove people from your life who make you feel awful and you're **not** a bad person for doing that. I was around people who made me feel so crap when I was at school, and I thought I was stuck with them forever. But they're not in my life anymore. Wahooooooo.

Friendships can be complicated, and I'm not saying that you can never have a row with a friend. Of course you can! But there's a massive difference between having a healthy friendship with normal ups and downs, and a toxic relationship where they make you feel bad about yourself. In your life, you'll lose friends and that's OK. There are always more people you can make friends with – I've learned that.

*So, stop holding on to a friendship if it's become poisonous – you deserve better than that.*

## Vampire friends

The last point in the box on the next page – when a friend never asks about you – is really the sign of a vampire friend. This is definitely one sort of friend you DO NOT NEED. EVER. They're called 'vampire friends' because that's what they do – they suck you dry! They're the person who just constantly bangs on about themselves, their dramas, but never asks anything about your life. (They probably don't even have a clue about what's going on with you AT ALL). You give them all your emotional energy, and they take it – without giving anything back.

I've seen so many vampire friends over the years – a couple that I've known and some that I've seen with other people. I've seen how damaging it is to your own mental health to be around someone like that. You end up feeling responsible for them, as they're always the ones who need the attention. They might call or text all the time, but it's only for things they want or need from you. It's a one-way street, and isn't really a friendship at all.

A good way to find out whether you have a vampire friend is to ask yourself: do you feel exhausted after you've spent time with this person? (and not the sort of tired when you've had a fun, massive night out, the sort of tired that wrecks your head and makes you feel empty inside). If so, then they're a vampire friend, and it's probably time to move on.

## WHEN YOU KNOW A FRIENDSHIP IS TOXIC

> They're dismissive towards your feelings

> They lie to you

> They take the p*ss out of you in front of other people to get attention

> They completely change their personality when they're around different people

> They're oblivious to how they make you feel

> They're always on their phone when they're with you

> They never ask how YOU'RE doing

# WHAT REAL FRIENDS SAY
# VS WHAT FAKE FRIENDS SAY

*Real Friend*

You should definitely apply for that job if you want it – go for it! What have you got to lose?

*Fake Friend*

Hmmm, are you really sure you're cut out for that sort of thing?

*Real Friend*

I'll come with you tonight, I know you need support.

*Fake Friend*

Look, I'm not sure if I'm free. I might text you later if nothing else is happening?

*Real Friend*

Please tell me how you're feeling. I want to help you.

*Fake Friend*

Sorry you're feeling crap, but OH MY GOD did you hear about my crazy day?

*Real Friend*

We all screw up and make mistakes. Don't worry about it.

*Fake Friend*

I can't believe you did that. You're such an idiot.

---

*Real Friend*

I promised you I wouldn't tell anyone and I never will.

*Fake Friend*

Look, I didn't mean to, but she got it out of me! It was impossible NOT to tell her . . .

*Real Friend*

What do you want to do for your birthday next week?

*Fake Friend*

It's your *birthday?*

---

## Avoiding negative energy

One thing I find really depressing is being around someone who's just relentlessly negative about other people. I'm not talking about when someone's going through some stuff and they NEED to get s**t off their chest. That's understandable. I'm more talking about a situation when you're hanging out with someone who likes to make negative comments about people they don't know. Like walking past someone in the street and saying something, like, 'What the hell is *she* wearing?' I really don't like that and don't want to be around people like that. It's just negative energy and it brings you down, as well as them.

I think I've become even more attuned to this since I've become well known. I've never liked that judginess anyway, but it's even worse when you've experienced it yourself. I know how bad it feels inside when you read a negative comment from someone who has no idea who you are.

It's hurtful and harmful to put that negative energy out there, whoever it's towards.

*FRIENDSHIP TRUTH #5:*
*the greatest gift you can give*
*somebody is your attention*

## Loving everyone's unique qualities

I'm so happy that I've got some incredible friends now, who I've been close with for years. They're amazing people who have stuck with me throughout it all, but they're all so different as well.

I think that's one of the lovely things about having a variety of friends – you have different mates for different moods and different times. Everyone's unique, so they bring those unique qualities with them, and bring out diverse aspects to our personalities, too. For example, if I want to have fun and party, I'm probably gonna call my friend Chelsey (who I met a few years ago when she did my hair). If I feel like being pampered at a spa day, I'll call Claire. If I need to talk to someone who knows me inside out, I'll call my sister Sam.

That's the great thing about having individual friends – you get different energies from them, and you do the same for them (even if you don't realise it). It doesn't mean you're being fake, it's just about that natural rapport you have with someone – you're probably more sociable with your more outgoing friend, and more thoughtful with a quieter friend. And that's OK.

*I think it's really important to remember that one friend can't give you EVERYTHING you need.*

They can't be the person who makes you laugh AND counsels you after a breakup AND parties with you all night AND then stays in with you when you just wanna chill AND gives you great career advice AND listens to you moan about whatever . . . that's impossible! A friend doesn't have to have every quality you need in a person – they just need to have a few. You can't put all that pressure on just *one* person.

## The roles we play in a group

Although I'm still more comfortable having one-on-one friendships, a lot of my friends know each other, so we do hang out as a group. And I've noticed that it's really easy to fall into a particular role when you're with lots of other people. I mean, we're not the f**king Spice Girls, just destined for one personality, but it's what happens!

**The wise one:** the person who's amazing at giving advice, and supporting other friends in standing up for themselves.
**The bodyguard:** the friend who wants to protect everyone else and fix their problems. They worry if anyone else is struggling, they don't like to see anyone feeling sad.
**The comedian:** always joking, they are brilliant fun and bring so much positive energy to a friendship group.
**The outspoken one:** this friend will always say exactly what's on their mind,

and will be completely honest with you. They're about as far away from two-faced as it's possible to be, and you can be sure of them.

**The free spirit:** this is the person you can call up at any time of day or night, and they'll be up for something! They have such a positive energy, and like to say yes to everything.

**The mother hen:** the mummy of the group! This person looks after everybody, is caring and super-nurturing. You know they'll always have your back.

## What I'm like as a friend

Sometimes it's hard to know how your friends see you – what we think on the inside often isn't what people see! The best and simplest way around this is to just ask your friends, and trust me, if they're a good friend, they'll send you a really supportive, honest and lovely message back.

I asked my friends Claire and Chelsey what kind of friend they think I am. It was actually really nice to hear what they thought of me (even though it felt strange to ask!). So I'd really recommend you do it, too. Here's their responses, along with my thoughts on what sort of friend I think I am.

### *According to me . . .*

I definitely think I'm the bodyguard in my friendship group! I want to fix everyone's problems. I want to be there for everyone, whenever they need me. I think that feeling got more intense when I got into my music career, because I didn't want my friends to think I'd changed. I'd feel like total crap if I wasn't there for someone when they needed me, even if I wasn't anywhere near them in the world.

I also never want anyone to be sad, which goes beyond friendships, that's how I feel about anyone, even a stranger – I want to fix their whole life. That's just me. I'm really protective over my friends, and when we hang out I'm always totally prepared to ask and find out what's going on with them, defend them if someone is rude to them and ask them, 'Who do I need to fight?' if they look sad . . .!

### *According to my friend Claire . . .*

'Initially, you were a hard nut to crack. I now know that this is due to s\*\*t people and experiences in your past, so it's a protective layer – but once you're in, you're in!

'You're always fiercely loyal and protective. You have real integrity and I love that about you, down to earth and real from the off. You won't let people close to you if they're not being authentic, so your group is small but solid.

'It's hard to describe our particular friendship as it's more like family. We have grown together, our friendship has changed and grown with us, which is amazing, as our lives have gone in different directions really.

'I think your vibe attracts your tribe and our similarities serve us well. We are honest and open with each other always, and it's wonderful to have a friend I trust with my life – and not just because you're a karate champion!

'Creative, humble, funny, compassionate and generous. The same qualities I think that have helped you with your career success are the qualities that make you a truly wonderful human and friend.'

### *According to my friend Chelsey . . .*

'Where to start? You're one of the most caring, kindest, funniest, most loveable humans ever. I know you would never judge me no matter what I'm about to say . . . I could come to you with anything and you'd listen and try to help me overcome whatever the issue is. You have my back if I ever need you to, but you wouldn't let people talk about me behind my back! You're trustworthy, you have the biggest heart. You're so much fun! Never a dull moment when I'm with you. You're also super-loyal.'

## WHAT YOU'RE LIKE AS A FRIEND

....................................................................................

....................................................................................

....................................................................................

....................................................................................

....................................................................................

....................................................................................

....................................................................................

....................................................................................

## My tattoos and what I've learned from my friends

My tattoos are really special to me, because they're written by my friends and whatever they've taught me. I simply got people to write certain words on me in their handwriting, and then they got copied over by the tattooist! They represent the amazing qualities all my friends have, and what I admire most in them.

forgiveness

*Forgiveness by Beanie:*

It all started with this one. Beanie forgives people really easily and I'm so jealous of that 'cause I just f**king hold a grudge forever! So I had this random thought a few years ago – I'll ask him to write 'forgiveness' on my shoulder, get it tattooed over, in the hope that I'll see it subconsciously and remember it. My thinking was, *Maybe if it's written on me then I'll learn from it.*

Once I had Beanie's one done, I thought I'd get other people to write what they've taught me, too. Now I have words all over me that the people closest to me have written. (The only one I did myself is the one saying 'Don't Panic!') But these are the others and why I have them . . .

*Confidence by Claire:*

I always felt like Claire was a confident woman in any situation. She's intelligent enough to always know the right thing to say, she never gets flustered. She always stands her ground, and I wanted to have that quality, too. She's taught me so much.

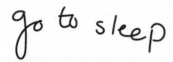

### Go to sleep by Jazz:

Jazz is my manager, and this is the phrase that most regularly comes out of her mouth. It's written on my hand, and back to front on purpose, so that if I look in the mirror when I brush my teeth I can read it properly! She's really well-read and is totally in tune with mental health. She's taught me the most about it on my own journey and is super-aware of everyone's emotions.

# HONESTY

### Honesty by Bridgette:

I always feel like Bridgette is never scared to tell the truth or stand up for what she believes in, no matter the consequences. I've learned a lot from her about that. Bridgette is someone that if she didn't like my outfit she'd be like, 'f**king take it off.' And that's what I love about her!

# Trust Think Twice

### Trust + Think twice by Kesi:

Kesi is one quarter of Rudimental and I've known him for years now. *Trust* is because I've never trusted a boy before, so that's simply about that. And the *Think twice* is a reminder to move past my gut instinct. In any situation I'll often have an instant/irrational thought that I go along with. And no matter if he agrees with me or not, he'll throw me the other side of the story, which I think is amazing. It's not about arguing with me, it's reminding me that OK, you may think something now, but just give it a moment before you make your mind up.

*Why not?*

**Why not? by Nicola:**

Nicola is always up for doing whatever, at any time. I met her when she came up to me and Claire after seeing our Motown show and asked to become part of the group. She will do whatever comes into her head, be spontaneous and seize the day. She kept me going out while I was trying to be a hermit. I could literally text her now and say, *What shall we do today*? This tattoo really reminds me of the importance of being spontaneous.

*Love*

**Love by Sam:**

This just encapsulates everything Sam is about. When I think about my sister, I just feel an overwhelming love – it's different from what I feel for anyone else. And she gives out so much love to everyone and I really love that about her.

*Speak your mind*

**Speak your mind by Donna:**

I met Donna through Claire and immediately liked her – she's really outspoken. This is where the idea for my first album title came from! She wrote it on my arm and at the album photoshoot, the photographer zoomed into it. We both saw the picture and said, *That's the name of the album!* Donna always speaks her mind, to an-y-one. She doesn't care. She does whatever she wants, whenever she wants. She lives by her own rules and I love that.

# BREAK THE RULES

**Break the rules by my godson, Sebastian:**
He's an amazing little human and loves to break and bend the rules. Which is a bit like me. I do the opposite of what I'm told to do, because I am like, *Who the hell made that rule up?* Even something as stupid as 'couches are made for sitting on', I'll think, I'm not going to sit on the couch, I'm like, *I'm going to sit on the floor!* He's a bit like that. He reminds me to carry on doing things my way.

# Family is everything ♡

**Family is everything by Mum:**
My mum is totally dedicated to her family. Even now, she's stopped working so she can look after my grandad, who's got dementia and Alzheimer's disease. She's so giving and generous. She reminds me that family is really important, and we should stay in touch with each other as much as we can.

# Don't Get a tattoo

**Don't get a tattoo by Dad:**
This is a funny one. My dad has NEVER wanted me to get any piercings or tattoos, ever – but he's got them! And my sister got one first. So I was like, Dad, how can you still say that? When I started getting my tattoos I thought it would be OK for him because it's sentimental, rather than a fashion thing. When I got this tattoo done, he just laughed.

*FRIENDSHIP TRUTH #6:*

*to be inherently kind is to be a good friend*

## A few words on . . . how to be a good friend

First of all, I feel like none of us can be the perfect friend ALL the time. That's not intentional, it's just that sometimes we have our own s\*\*t going on. In the same way that we should cut our own friends some slack from time to time, we need to do the same for ourselves.

*We're human, we make mistakes.*

I definitely am guilty of making mistakes. And I've learned that at times I haven't checked in on my friends enough. But my intention was always good. So I think as long as you are thinking about them and doing your best to check in on them as much as you can, then you're doing well.

At the heart of it, I think the most important thing is to just be inherently kind. Just be a decent, kind human with good morals, and then you'll be a good friend.

When you have really good friends, it feels as natural as breathing. If you haven't found those people yet, don't worry. It took me some time. Eventually you'll find your people and never feel out of place with them. Let it happen naturally. Just concentrate on you.

I thought / love was
the answer to all of
my problems

# Betrayal, toxic boys and discovering what makes a real relationship

**S**o, this is how we're all told a relationship goes. Boy meets girl. They fall in love, get married and live happily ever after (maybe with a dance number chucked in for good measure, too). Right? No? But that's what happened in every single movie romcom and musical that I watched growing up . . . and I thought it would happen to me too. What an idiot.

I'm not completely taking the p*ss:

*I definitely based my idea of relationships on the movies and shows I watched.*

I loved movies like *The Notebook*, and Disney ones like *Cinderella*, *Snow White* and *The Little Mermaid*, which were amazing films but DEFINITELY gave me unrealistic expectations of how relationships work. They were full of 'perfect' moments, beautiful people and idealised love stories, and

I couldn't wait to have that myself. Not only that, but my mum and dad had got together when they were only fourteen – so I expected that I'd have the same experience, too.

These expectations meant I grew up with a totally weird idea of what relationships would look like: I'd meet the love of my life at school, and that would be that. (Cue the end-of-credits music). Of course, it didn't quite work out like that, but having that rose-tinted mentality didn't serve me very well, either.

## My first experiences of boys

My first 'proper' relationship was probably Jamie, who I went out with in Year 9 (and you all know by now how well *that* ended). I wasn't in love with him, or anything like that. He was interesting, and I was intrigued by the different lives we had growing up. He was a totally different character to anyone I'd known. And I liked that.

This relationship would set the bar for what I'd expect for every future relationship. And, as you can guess, that bar was set pretty f**king low. When we split up I was left with no self-confidence. There went the dream of meeting the person I was going to spend the rest of my life with at school.

## New relationships, but old expectations

At college I met a boy – we'll call him Daniel – who I fell for. He was funny and he made me laugh a lot, which was a new thing for me. It taught me something positive about what a relationship could be. We had loads of fun together, but he was still a bit of a pr*ck.

*He cheated on me, and he didn't treat me well at all – things that I shouldn't have put up with, but I did.*

'Cause that's what I thought relationships were like.

I remember one time when I was seventeen, I was waiting for him to pick me up from home so we could go out. I sat there dressed up and ready. I'd told Mum and Dad he was coming, but he didn't turn up. He didn't answer his phone or reply to any of my texts. He didn't even tell me he wasn't coming, he just didn't show. It was humiliating. But because I was so emotionally buttoned-up at this point, I couldn't be honest about how upset I was. Mum asked if he was still picking me up and I lied and said I'd changed our plans and pretended I was fine. I wouldn't let anyone see how hurt I was. Instead I silently cried into my pillow in my room. I was, and still am, a very sensitive person.

The way he treated me made me feel insecure. But I stayed with him because I still had that hope that he was the person I might marry and be with for the long run. We eventually broke up when we were in the second year of college. I found out he cheated and to be honest, I think he was treating me bad so I would finish it with him, 'cause he didn't have the bollocks to do it himself.

## Feeling lost and putting up with crappy treatment

After that experience, I went a bit off the rails. I was wild. I was really directionless and had no idea what I was gonna do with my life. I'd left college, but I didn't have a job, and it was a really low period for me.

# *I didn't care about myself, so I expected nothing from other people.*

It wasn't any wonder that the boys who I was with then were f**kheads.

I had such a damaging view of what to expect in a relationship. I'd built up a really negative picture of what I thought *all* boys were like. In my mind, this concept was totally normal: boys would treat you bad, and you put up with it. I get it now, that's what *some* boys were like. But it doesn't mean that's what's RIGHT, that's what all boys are like, or what any of us deserve. But, back then, that's what I thought I needed to be like in a relationship – give boys whatever they wanted and then they'd stay with me forever. It was never about what they would do for me, being loyal, supporting me or sticking up for me. I never got deep with anyone, or expected better for myself. What a mess.

## From perfect guy to controlling cheater

A few years later, I fell in love for the first time. I was doing the talent shows, and it was at one of those that I met Matthew, who I've mentioned before – he was the one that Claire helped me get over. He was a drummer in a band, talented and really clever. He was from East London, which felt like a totally different world from the one I was used to (although it was only a few miles away!) Again, I was intrigued by the differences between us. He taught me loads about history, about politics, about geography – stuff I knew nothing about. I was self-admittedly obsessed.

I thought it was the perfect relationship for so long. We were madly in love, and never wanted to be apart. He made me feel wanted, which was very different to what I'd felt before – I thought, *This is it! This is the person who I want to get married to!*

But then things started to get a bit weird. Bit by bit, he started trying to change the way I dressed, criticising me for wearing lipstick and stuff like that. He'd see me with my friends, laughing and joking, but afterwards he would say, 'Who was that person you were just now?' He was freaked out by it, because I was a different person with my friends – loud and outgoing. To be honest, he never saw the person I really was. He wanted me to be different.

*But I was too in love to see straight. I changed around him.*

I acted differently. Whatever he wanted, I'd give him. I'd wear what he wanted me to wear, and listen to music he wanted us to listen to. Obviously, in hindsight I see now how I allowed that spiral to happen – I wanted to do anything that would make him happy.

## WHAT A SUPPORTIVE PARTNER WOULD NEVER SAY IN A MILLION YEARS

'Are you sure you want to eat that?'

'You look better without make-up – don't put it on.'

'I like you better with long hair. It's more feminine.'

'Going out wearing that? Really?'

'My ex used to . . .'

'What are you making me for dinner, then?'

## Betrayed, but still trapped

One night at one of his gigs, I noticed a particular girl there, and she started popping up all the time after that. I felt suspicious instantly – that was my gut instinct again – but he swore blind she was just a random girl. I wasn't so sure. So later that week, when I was round there for the evening, on my own in his room, I logged on to his emails on his laptop. (I was a detective wannabe, too, as you know).

The first thing I saw was a message from her saying, 'I miss you, when can we talk? My heart dropped like a stone, I was like, *What the f\*\*k?* I went onto MSN and clicked 'save conversations' – I knew that this would save chats into a document form once you logged out. My plan was to confront him about it, then hope he would go onto MSN and talk to her and that would be my evidence. So that's what I did, I confronted him. And on the spot, he claimed that it was a totally innocent friendship – her mum and dad were breaking up and he was just 'being there for her' (It's pretty scary to think how easily and quickly he came up with that lie.) Anyway, I told him that I believed him, but that I wanted him to call her after I'd slept to see what the vibe was between them. He agreed and I slept. And I waited for my plan to unfold.

I did sleep a little but when I woke up, I went downstairs. He was playing FIFA so I grabbed the laptop and went on the other couch. BAM. My plan had worked. It was there – a message to this girl, telling her that I'd seen their messages and warning her about the phone call telling her to fake a conversation to reassure me nothing was going on. He even signed off the message to her: 'I'm so sorry this has to happen to you. *Te amo.*' It was like a moment from a film – I couldn't believe it. I was reading this conversation while he played FIFA just a few feet away from me.

I was shaking with rage and anger. We had a row – I completely flipped out. When we both eventually calmed down, we had a conversation. 'Well, obviously we're over because I'm not going to deal with you now,' I said. He looked heartbroken. 'I can't lose you, I will never talk to her again,' he promised.

I can't quite believe this now but after all that WE STAYED TOGETHER. I know it sounds crazy, but back then I thought I had good reasons. One reason was because of this ideal that I had in my head of meeting someone and staying with them forever. Secondly, because my self-esteem was SO low – I thought that it was better to stay with him because maybe everyone cheats and you just stay with one person and put up with their mistakes. And thirdly? Because I hoped I could change him. I know now you can't judge people by your own standards.

To be honest, I should have let him go, but I couldn't bring myself to do it.

*I thought I would be worse off on my own than with him – I was wrong.*

The relationship dragged on. He went off to college, and I'd travel up to see him regularly. But he gradually became a different person. He had a new bunch of friends and I remember thinking, *This is not me, I don't fit in here.* I did try though. Tried dressing like them, talking like them, listening to the same music. But even then, the more I tried to become the person I thought he wanted me to be, the nastier he was. It was like he actually hated me.

It all came to a head one time when I drove up to surprise him. He literally stood on his front door step and told me to turn around and go home. He wouldn't let me in. He didn't want me there. Thinking back now, he probably had another girl in there. Yuk. I felt pathetic. I just thought, *What is wrong with me? I haven't done anything wrong? Everyone is just horrible to me all the time. It must be me.*

## Building myself back up through heartbreak

Finally, that toxic relationship, which had sucked away years of my life, was over. But I didn't feel great about it for a long time. I felt like absolute s**t, to be honest. It was after that incident that I drove to Claire's. She said, 'I am not letting you leave this house, you are not going back there.' Over the next few months, I let out all my crying and started to heal. I was still obsessed with him, so I had to force myself to block him from every form of social media and delete his number. As time gradually went on, I began to return to myself. It was Claire that got me better, really.

It wasn't the last time I saw him, though. I did have one last great f**k-you moment. He came back from college and got in touch, telling me he really wanted to see me. I wasn't sure whether it was the right thing to do, but I agreed, and drove over to meet with him. Seeing him after so long was shocking. I had a completely different perception of him. All of a sudden, he looked ugly to me. His eyes, his nose, his teeth – everything looked different, although of course, *he* hadn't changed at all. I had.

He wanted to give it another go and get back together. But this time, *I didn't want him.* I realised in that moment, *F**king hell, I'm actually over you!* I was like, 'No thanks! See ya.' I dropped him off home and left. It was so brilliant to have that feeling.

## IF YOU'RE FEELING HEARTBROKEN. . . BREAKUP SONGS TO MAKE YOU FEEL BETTER

Erykah Badu – 'Tyrone'

Cardi B – 'Be Careful'

Lauryn Hill – 'Nothing Even Matters'

Alicia Keys – 'A Woman's Worth'

Kelly Rowland feat. Beyoncé & Michelle – 'You Changed'

Ray BLK – 'Lovesick'

UPSAHL – 'Douchebag'

Avelino – 'FYO'

Frankee – 'F.U.R.B'

## What I was like as a girlfriend

You can probably tell from all these dramas that up until my twenties, I didn't have great relationship experiences. Being treated like s\*\*t and cheated on made me insecure and fed into how I behaved as a girlfriend and how I felt about how I looked. I was really needy and jealous. I'd tell my partners not to look at other girls, and demand they focus more on me. I desperately craved their attention, whatever the cost, and for them to tell me things were OK. I was in constant need of their love and approval.

Apart from me being totally annoying (which I know I was), I understand now this attitude came from a really bad place inside.

*I had a damaging mentality where I thought I had to stay with people, that I couldn't get anyone better than them.*

That I didn't deserve any better. That I needed to do what they wanted, not what I wanted to do. It was terrible, and really unhealthy.

I've spoken to my therapist about how I was in relationships, and she described it as taking on the 'lapdog' role. It's where one person does whatever the other person wants, just to try to make them happy, in an attempt to stop them from leaving. She was so right – I hadn't ever thought about what *I* wanted, I didn't really care. I just wanted the other person to be happy. My mindset was: *I'll be whoever they want me to be and then they'll never leave me.*

It was wrong, and so exhausting. And quite obviously didn't work. It wasn't really who I was elsewhere, either. To the people that knew me, I was a free spirit, confident and happy as I toured the world and sang in front of thousands. But in a relationship I was a completely different person. A mug.

## Working things out through music

To be honest, the reason I started writing about my relationships in my music was that it was the easiest way for me to write a song. In the early days of my career, I tried for so long to write lyrics about other things, things that I hadn't experienced. I'd sit there for ages, thinking, *What do I write about? I can't think of anything I wanna say.* Things that I wrote back then were just a load of old bollocks, really, it wasn't me at all. The songs reflected that, 'cause they were crud.

I remember being in a session and someone asking me, 'Have you had a bad relationship lately? How do you feel at the moment?' It was quite nerve-wracking answering those questions, but we started having conversations about things I'd gone through, and the words just flowed out of me. It felt really easy and so good to do this, too, because up until then, I hadn't been able to tell anyone about all the crap I'd experienced.

*I wouldn't always realise, though, how close my lyrics were to the actual truth.*

While I was in the process of writing them down, it would feel like a story I was separate from, and it turned gradually into a song. It wouldn't be until a few weeks or months after recording it that I would sit there listening back and think, *F\*\*king hell, that is word for word the situation I went through!* It was like a whirlwind, I didn't realise what I'd got out of my system until much later on when I was listening back.

As I started to become more honest in my music, it felt really easy to write, because it was real. It was instinctive and natural: I knew how I felt and thought about these things, because I'd gone through them. And it soon became my 'thing' – me, my life and my music were intertwined. It was my conscious decision to talk about what I felt and that felt really good. I thought, if I've gone through this, surely other people will have too.

If I'm being honest, there was a satisfying element to writing my lyrics, too. As I got more successful, I did wonder a couple of times whether my exes would hear those songs on the radio and realise that they were about them . . . I've no idea if they have, though (although if they have . . . HA HA HA!)

# THE STORIES BEHIND THE SONGS

**'Ciao Adios':** this is about my ex, Matthew, and how hard it was to say goodbye. I finally got up the courage to tell him to eff off in that car, so I thought, *How many times can I say bye in one song?* and that was the idea of saying it in different languages! I just wanted to say goodbye as much as possible.

**'Alarm':** it's about when I was with someone who'd left their girlfriend to be with me, so I spent the whole relationship worried they would do the same to me. It's about that feeling of *Oh s\*\*t, it's happening to me* – that the karma comes around. That's where the line 'taxed him from his ex' comes from – he's doing the same to me as he did to her.

**'Some People':** this was about coming out of a relationship with an ex who acted single even when he was with me. He was with someone else while we were together. Sometimes you love someone more than they love you and they're not going to treat you as well as you deserve.

Songwriting has helped me so much because it forced me into a place where I had to talk about *something.* Initially I didn't even realise it was helping me, it was just stuff that was coming out of my head. It took me going through therapy to realise how much it helped me process my emotions and work through things and now I'm really aware of how much it helps.

You don't have to write lyrics to help you process your emotions – whatever it is that helps get them out of your head is good! My sister Sam writes a diary, which she says really helps her get it all out. You could record a video, draw, write notes – whatever it is, it's something that releases those thoughts from your head and puts them somewhere else. It means you can move on from those feelings instead of letting them fester inside.

## Good relationships and what they're about

It was while writing a song recently that I had an epiphany about who I'm with now. I was chatting with the other songwriters in the studio, telling them I wanted to write about what it feels like to be with someone and realising you don't *need* them anymore. This feeling worried me, because I'd never felt it before. Not needing someone, but *wanting* them instead. I'd made that shift from feeling like you need that person to boost you up and keep you going, to feeling stronger and actually just *wanting* them to be in your life. A change of mindset from negative to positive.

After the song was complete, I thought, *Oh, god, do I tell him that? That I don't need him anymore?* I was worried to tell him to be honest, 'cause if someone had told *me* that a few years ago I would have died. But I thought I'd show him the song and explain that this is how I feel – I don't need you anymore, I simply just want you. His response was, 'That's brilliant, that's the way it should be.' He was really pleased for me to have that realisation. I'm lucky that he's not full of bravado and insecurity. He's happy that I'm happy.

Our relationship has changed and evolved over time. At the start I was just like I was before – needy, anxious and a bit of a lapdog. If I'm honest, I was a bit worried that he wouldn't wanna be with the person I've become, because I'm different from the person he fell in love with. But he reassures me that my new-found me only makes everything better, including our relationship. I'm more confident and do what makes me happy. For example, if we're at home and chatting about what we're gonna do that night, I used to say, 'Whatever you want to do.' Now, I say what I want. But it's all good.

*We're a relationship of equals, now. We keep communicating, we keep explaining, we keep sharing how we feel.*

A proper, actual relationship.

I have learned over time what makes a good relationship. And one of the biggest things I've learned is that a partner isn't the other half of you. You are not half a person and someone else fills the other half to make you whole.

*You don't need to have another half. You are a whole person all by yourself.*

A good partner will just add on to that. Realising that was HUGE for me because it's so different to how I used to feel and think before.

## THE TRUEST THINGS I'VE READ ABOUT LOVE

> Always trust actions over words

> Repeated mistakes aren't accidents

> You shouldn't hold on to something just because you have history together

> If you don't appreciate me at my worst you definitely don't deserve me at my best

> You're not being selfish for wanting to be treated well

> The moment that you start to wonder whether you deserve better, you do

## When I realised I could be in control

I remember having a conversation once when I was about twenty-five that changed my whole brain on the dynamics in relationships. I was out with a group of mates, and we were all chatting about why people lie in general. Cause you know, I *hate* liars. One guy said, 'Boys lie all the time. It's up to how their partner is feeling at that moment whether they believe the lies or not.'

That blew my mind and I'd never thought about it from that perspective before. There have been times where I've felt so s**t about myself and been so needy, that if someone lied to me I'd be like, *OK, I believe you,* *let's move past it.* (Which was pretty much what happened with Matthew). Whereas if they told me the *same* lie on a day I was feeling confident and loved myself, I'd be like, *F\*\*k off, you lying prick!*

This perspective shift made me understand that I wasn't going to be able to change the person I was with – if they were a liar, they were a liar. It was up to me to figure myself out, to accept or not accept this person and how they treated me, create my own standards, and that had a direct link to how good I felt about myself.

*I also realised: maybe it wasn't me all along, maybe they were just arseholes.*

Back when I was seventeen, and putting up with all sorts of rubbish from boys, I couldn't even *fathom* having that point of view in a relationship. It wouldn't have even occurred to me that I could consider that he was the one being the d\*ck, and that I could tell him to do one.

## Why you deserve better

I know how hard it is to get out of a relationship even when it's not healthy. I did it myself – I stayed with people that didn't deserve me, that didn't treat me right. So I understand it when it takes people time to get out of these situations. It's really hard to do when you're in the thick of it.

*It can sometimes feel impossible to get out of a toxic relationship, especially if you love that person (and even if you don't).*

There's a great phrase I read somewhere about love: *it's gonna hurt me to let go but loving you is worse.* That was the situation with Matthew – I was in so much pain with him, but I thought leaving him would be a million times worse. That was why I stayed with him. It's so hard to move on. But it is possible to do.

So don't be hard on yourself *(did you hear Jess Glynne singing that, or is that just me?)* If you had a crappy relationship in the past, or if you're still in one now. Be forgiving if you didn't get out of it straight away. Look, I'm realistic. It took me time to learn what I deserved – I didn't just read a few inspirational quotes on Pinterest and then go, *Rah, that's me all sorted with relationships now* . . . It took a long while, and sorting out all the other issues I've dealt with, to understand how I should be treated by a partner.

For me, a lot of stuff got put into perspective too, when I thought about how short our lives really are. When you think about it, at most, we're gonna have no more than eighty or ninety years on this earth. And that got me thinking, why the hell am I wasting time feeling like this in this relationship? Feeling sad and wondering whether it's all there is? Realising how much of my short life bad relationships were taking up has made me think twice. Life is precious.

It's OK to be single. It's OK to get divorced. It's OK to move on. It's OK to be married. It's OK not to be married. It's OK to have children. It's OK not to have children.

*What's not OK is staying in a relationship where you're not valued and appreciated.*

## How to help a friend in a s\*\*tty relationship

Sometimes it's not you that's in the bad place, it's someone else. And that can be hard in its own way. The nightmare situation is when someone asks for your help in dealing with a crappy partner, you give them your honest opinion (badmouthing their partner and saying you think they're a massive loser), but then they end up getting back together and afterwards feel like they can't talk to you about their relationship anymore . . . OUCH.

It happens. But I've learned over time how to try to be diplomatic in these circumstances, rather than just getting REALLY angry on someone else's behalf (which I used to do). It's hard, but it is possible. So, here's what I've learned:

**1** If they're asking you for advice at the start of a relationship, then that's your get-out-of-jail-free card. They're probably not that invested in it yet, so you can be **more honest** in how you react to what they tell you.

**2** If they're asking you for advice in the thick of an established relationship, don't rush to speak, **just listen.** And rather than bombarding them with your opinion, ask questions and ask them what they think about their partner's behaviour.

**3** If they haven't asked for your advice, then **tread carefully.** Again, don't go steaming in with your opinion (however right you think you are). Offer to chat about the situation when your friend is ready to, and if they're up for it, encourage them to be more reflective about their own situation. Take yourself and your thoughts out of the equation!

It's hard, but you've got to let friends figure things out for themselves. I was the same – it took me all my therapy and songwriting to realise how bad some of my relationships had gotten. Sometimes I'd literally listen back to songs a few weeks after recording them and think, *Oh my god, I need to sort it out.*

# THE ONE QUESTION TO ASK YOURSELF ABOUT ANY RELATIONSHIP

OK, so I love this. If you're not sure about your own relationship, if you're in that place where you can't really be certain whether it's the right thing for you, whether they're treating you well enough or not – whatever it is, I understand. It's really hard to see the wood for the trees sometimes. So just ask yourself this one, easy question:

> *What would you say to a friend if they were going through the same thing?*

This really seems to help everyone get clarity and go, *huh*. Because then you start to see things from the outside in.

Think about it. If your friend told you the *exact same situation* that you are going through right now, but they were experiencing it rather than you, what would your reaction be? Would you think their partner was decent? OK? Supportive? Just going through a difficult time? Or would you think they were manipulative? Controlling? Cruel? A total waste of space?

If you wouldn't want your friend to have a partner like that, then you shouldn't have a partner like that, either. You deserve better, ffs.

For me, it all comes down to the power of talking (again!) Sometimes you don't realise how f\*\*ked up someone is treating you until you're explaining it to someone else. Do you know what I mean? It's easy to not realise how bad things are if nobody else knows about it. It's only when you talk about it to someone else and see their reaction that you can see how shocking the situation really is.

*So, talk to each other. Don't judge too much. Listen. Be open.*

Help yourself and the friends around you get the relationships you all deserve. Remember how amazing you are (because you are). Once you feel good enough about yourself, being good enough for somebody else will be the least of your concerns.

# PART 2

# Now, Take On The World

've always been a very strong-minded person. I know what I like, and how I want things to be. But this used to be only on the inside. Until recently, I found it hard to be vocal about my feelings and thoughts on the outside. I'd push them down deep within myself for fear of how others would react. I'd flex, and twist and turn at work to make sure everyone else was happy and didn't think I was a 'diva'. I'd wear clothes because other people told me they looked better than the ones I liked to wear. I'd pretend I didn't care about negative stuff people said about me online. I was constantly wrapped up in 'people pleasing'.

I thought I would be letting other people down, but the only person I was actually letting down was myself.

I'm not like that now, though. I've learned how to be myself on the outside, as well as the inside.

Changing who I am to make other people happy only leaves me feeling unhappy and unworthy to be myself. I was always so nice and flexible for people that they'd be OK with mugging me off, 'cause they knew I'd be 'all right' about it. But it's bollocks –

*faking who you are on the outside only makes you feel like s**t on the inside.*

It's something so many of us do ALL the time: putting on a false front because we're trying to be something or someone else. We're so influenced by what others' opinions and society tells us to be that often, we lose sight of what's real. We're not truly ourselves.

So, this part of the book is all about that: getting rid of the fake fronts we can all put on, and learning how to be completely comfortable with who we are, so we can make decisions for ourselves.

*Because this is about taking up our place in the world: whether that's with our careers, our personal style or how we communicate and relate to others online.*

It's all the stuff that people see about us, the way the world views us, and the stuff that we often (mis)judge with others, too.

## Why we need to change

I know that I used to be like this. I used to think I was the only one with any problems, because I only saw what people showed on the surface. I thought everyone else was way happier than me because of how they presented themselves online and IRL. I didn't think that anyone else had any issues – apart from cases where it was really bloody obvious they did! I fell into the trap of getting sucked into only looking at the surface stuff – other people's jobs, their achievements, how stunning they looked, blah blah – and feeling like crap in comparison to them.

But I've learned this isn't the whole story. It's only a tiny part.

Because to some extent, we're all faking how we present ourselves. We're being who we think people want us to be; we make decisions we think others want us to make. I used to do it. I'd always wanted to be liked so I used to put out energy that I thought people would want from me. But it was so stressful, being like that, and took so much effort. And it didn't help at all – not me or anyone else.

In fact, the more and more I've been myself, the more people have naturally liked me. I *never* thought that would happen! I was convinced for years that people wouldn't like my true personality, but once I started to let it bubble through, I realised, *actually this is OK*. It also meant I liked myself a lot more, because there was no disconnect between who I was, inside and out. And that felt really good.

## Redefining our outer selves

So, in the first half of the book, we looked deep inside at our emotions, our mental health and all the stuff that others can't know about us from the outside. All the things they can't see. But in this section, we're going to talk about the things they do see – the outside you – and, actually, how it MASSIVELY relates to the inside! How to find something you love to do. How to express yourself through what you wear. How to find a happy balance with how you relate to others online. And I'm going to share with you how I did it (messily, with lots of cock-ups) and how shifting my attitude has helped me (LOADS).

It's all about what we're putting out into the world, and making sure it tallies up with who we really are, deep down. Being comfortable with who you are. And I want to help you do it, because you can't do it alone. Are you superhuman? NO. I'm here with you.

Alright, this is your time / Time for your life to be yours

# Making it in music, the moments that changed my life and what I learned along the way

O K, so picture the scene. I'm eight years old, sitting on my knees at the edge of the stage at the Palace Theatre in London. I'm performing in the musical *Les Misérables* and dressed as the poor orphan Little Cosette, in a ragged brown dress, with make-up smeared all over my face, and my hair messed up. I'm about to sing my big song, 'Castle on a Cloud', and as the music strikes up, I am SO excited, in a way I haven't been for ages. I'm excited because I've decided to sing the song differently tonight – I'm gonna sing it in my own style.

I've been practising in my room at home, singing the song with my own natural voice tone, with my own inflections, rather than putting on the 'musical voice' that I've done in every performance up to now. I'd just randomly had the thought to do it in my own style, and I'm sure that the show producers are gonna be really impressed when they hear me sing it like this. I know my voice sounds better this way. I open my mouth, and start to sing . . .

You can see where this is going, can't you?

Yep, they were pretty pissed off! Far from being happy with me, after my performance the next day, I got told off. I was pulled back by the resident directors to have a chat.

'Are you OK – what happened last night? Why did you sing it like that?' they asked. Although I totally knew why (it was because I wanted to) I was too embarrassed to admit that so I covered up, saying, 'Oh I don't know.' They told me to sing it again in front of them to make sure I didn't do that again and to sing it the way I was supposed to. Back in your box, Anne-Marie. I was totally deflated – after all, I thought they'd love it.

I learned from that experience that being yourself wasn't something that was really allowed in the musical theatre world – it's very regimented. But I get it: you're playing a character, and the shows are written to be performed in a certain way. Being so young, it was my first taste of realising that I couldn't be myself, I couldn't express myself in the way I wanted to. You either had to do things a certain way, or not at all.

It was confusing. At the time, I was too young to really understand that this was a big sign that musical theatre really wasn't destined to be my future. But, looking back, I can see now how important that moment was for me. Not that I had *any* clue what my future was going to hold when I was eight – or even what I wanted to be – but doing something where I had to be the same as everyone else who'd come before me wasn't ever going to work.

*It was the moment I realised that I knew I wanted to do things my way.*

And actually, that's how it's felt throughout my career. Rather than a straightforward, linear story, my career journey has actually been more like a series of moments. Moments in time where I've learned something, been given a new insight or opportunity. Sometimes it's when I've been taught something incredible, or moments where I've almost lost it all.

But in every case I've taken something from it, something really valuable that I can share with you. These are the career moments that made me.

## The moment I learned you need to have passion

To be honest, I really didn't have a clue what to do after finishing my GSCEs, but I had to make a decision. That whole time was so weird and scary – the idea that I had to decide on my future NOW freaked me out. Because of this, I chose the obvious option, and went with what I knew: musical theatre. I thought it was the only thing I *could* do, so I enrolled in BTEC Performing Arts at college.

I had fun during those two years, and met some good people, but at the end of the course I didn't feel like it was right for me. One reason was I didn't think I'd be the best – which was quite f\*\*king shallow, I admit – but I knew my voice sounded different to the others on my course. I couldn't reach really high notes and back then I thought my range sounded more like a boy's range. I knew I wasn't as good as other people, and I wouldn't get the roles I wanted. I also knew I didn't really *care* – I had no passion for it as a career. Or for anything as a career at that moment, to be honest.

I had to do something and earn some money, so I got a part-time job at Ted Baker at House of Fraser at Lakeside Shopping Centre, just on weekends. I worked with some nice new people, so I stayed there for a while, before I went on to the restaurant Wagamama. I struggled with learning the menu by heart (which seemed to be a necessity) so I explained this to them, but their reply was that I HAD to learn it. I really couldn't, so I quit after three weeks. After that came Kidspace, a soft play venue. That was really fun, but still, I didn't care about turning up late and being told off. I remember once turning up (late) and the manager saying, 'Anne-Marie, you have so much potential, if you tried a little harder you would have a great career here . . .' I quit the next day.

From this point, I fell into a s**ty, directionless hole. I basically stayed at home from that moment on. I was an actual bum, I did *nothing*. I wasted hours on the Internet, reading up on conspiracy theories and becoming obsessed with this website called StumbleUpon. It was a really old-style search engine, where you'd click a button and get sent to any random page on the Internet. You'd flip from something like back massages to watching someone do a long jump – it was totally absorbing. I must have spent *weeks* on that website. If not months!

My parents must've been like, 'What the hell, Anne-Marie?' I'd gone from someone who was really focused on musical theatre and karate, to someone who had no motivation, nothing to get up for in the morning. I'd had those part-time jobs but no idea of what my life was truly gonna become.

It was then that I started doing those local talent shows, and I actually even auditioned for *The X Factor*, too. I went along with my dad, and I got through the first few rounds, which were off camera. Once I got to the point where you sing in front of the producers, they even said to me, 'We're gonna put you through, but can you show us that you *actually* want it?' It seemed that to everyone else I was just lazy and didn't care about anything (but in reality, it was because I was too scared of failing that I just never tried in the first place).

I had *completely* lost my way. It was a bad time.

*But what I learned was that it's so important to do something you're really into.*

I've never wanted to stick at something I didn't feel 100 per cent passionate about. When I knew something was right, I could roll with it, but if it wasn't right, I wasn't interested.

*WorkLife Lesson: find something that excites you, something that you are genuinely interested in doing. If you don't care about your career, you'll hate it and it won't make you happy. It's not just about money, it's about how it makes you feel when you get up in the morning.*

## The moment the door opened into music

It's weird when you look back, and can see the *Sliding Doors* moments in your life – those little moments that actually set you on a totally different path. Because often, they don't seem as if they're these big, massive moments at the time. It's not like in the movies – it's only with hindsight that you can see how important they were. And this was exactly how it was for me, when the door opened a crack into music.

It came out of a really random encounter. A boy that I'd been at college with was teaching this lady piano. Her name was Mary, she was a songwriter and she'd asked him if he knew any girls who could sing, because she wanted to record the songs she was writing. He asked me whether I'd be interested, and all I thought was, *Oh that sounds fun, I'll go and see if she wants me to do it.* I had literally no idea whether this was a big thing or not, and to be honest I didn't give it a second thought.

I met Mary, she liked my voice and we ended up working together on and off for a couple of years. She was older than me and had some experience in the music industry – she'd wanted to be an artist herself, so she knew a lot more than me. At the time I didn't have a clue, still, about either the music industry or what I wanted to do. But working with her was interesting and I had fun singing in a big studio in London.

She was the first person who I not only wrote a song with, but who asked me what sort of songs I wanted to sing. I guess that question made me start to think of myself as an artist. But even then I didn't take it that seriously. It was just a bit of fun to me. At the time I thought I'd wanna make really weird left-field stuff, because that was the music I was listening to – Grizzly Bear and Enter Shikari, stuff like that. But she said, 'If you want to make that kind of music you have to make more popular stuff first to get well known; after that you can do the music you like.' I was a bit frustrated by that at the time, because pop wasn't cool in the group I was hanging out with. (But obviously, I grew to love it!)

Recording with Mary at a London studio also started to lead to some unexpected opportunities. She had a music manager, who heard me sing. We worked together a bit and after a while he wanted me to come in for an interview at Sony Records: 'Come in tomorrow, sing a top ten song from the charts and I'll get you in a girl band,' he said. *Nah,* I thought, *I don't want to be in a girl band.* But there was also a vocal engineer at the studio, who liked my voice, and recommended me to another manager at the company. And that ended up leading to a lot more.

*WorkLife Lesson: you never, ever know where opportunities*
*will come from. It's not always from the obvious places, like getting on*
*a course, or landing a certain job. So, say yes to the random things that*
*might come your way, take a chance on something new.*
*Even if you're not sure what's in it for you straight away,*
*you never know where things might lead.*

## The moment I nearly lost it all – and learned to work harder

Things were starting to happen. Another manager from that management company took me on, and all of a sudden, I was being taken to meetings, and being put into songwriting sessions with people to see if I could produce anything good. They were testing me out, seeing if I was worth their time. But I carried on living and being as I was before – hanging out with my boyfriend at the time and performing sixties songs in the Motown show with my friend Claire. We were called The Motown Sisters, and we'd perform an hour's set of Motown and more modern songs at venues around Essex – holiday parks, pubs and clubs. I had to wear a sixties-style outfit: a black beehive wig, a black tassel-y dress, black heels, red silk gloves and a red headband. To be honest, I always got a bit nervous about performing, because it was me being someone else again, rather than myself. Before each show I had to neck down a WKD so I could go out there! (In fact, doing this show ended up really helping me train my voice in the long run, as I had to reach some really high notes.). But when it came to my new solo artist music career? To be honest, I wasn't really trying.

The management company couldn't believe it. 'You need to move to London, socialise with people in the music industry and not do the Motown show anymore,' they said. I was like, 'F**k off, I'm not quitting the Motown show and I'm staying in Essex!' They told me that if I wanted to make it, I had to forget about everything else and just focus on music. Like, *this is your life now*. But I didn't want to do that, it scared me, so I didn't. I was still stuck in the way I'd been at college – a bit naughty, a bit rude. People said I was talented, but I had an attitude problem.

But then I got a huge wake-up call.

I met Arthur Smith, a songwriter and producer, who is now one of my favourite humans ever. He could see that I was struggling to make my mark, and was confused by my attitude. Why wasn't I writing five songs a day? Why wasn't I turning up early for sessions? Actually, why wasn't I even turning up *on time?*

One day he gave me a pep talk. 'Less talented people are going to get further than you, because they work harder,' he told me. At the time, my response was IMPOSSIBLE! NO WAY! How could that happen? Why would less talented people do better? It just didn't make any sense.

And then, over time, I started seeing it happen and I was like, *Oh s\*\*t, he's right!* It was the first time I thought to myself, *Actually, yeah, I really don't try hard enough and look at what's happening. So, let's see what happens when I work harder.*

I started saying yes to more opportunities that he put my way. He'd ask whether I wanted to go to the studio, and I'd say yes and try to be on time! I wanted to make him proud. He was trying so hard to help me be successful and I felt like I owed it to him to try. He took me under his wing and taught me everything that I needed to know (which was a lot, BTW). He was such a good mentor to me.

I know I didn't really try my hardest at the start of my music career. I think a part of me didn't actually believe it was possible for me to become a successful singer, so I kind of self-sabotaged. I didn't want to try too hard and then fail, because that would be worse, wouldn't it? That was my problem. People saw it as a lack of motivation, but I was actually just too scared to try. Through nearly losing my chance, I learned one of the most important lessons I've ever learned, which was that I needed to work hard.

*Things didn't start really happening for me until I put that fear aside, and put the effort in.*

*WorkLife Lesson: things don't always come easy.*
*It might look like that from the outside, but most people who achieve*
*their goals do so because they've worked f\*\*ing hard to get there. If you*
*really want something, you've got to put in the hours and the effort to*
*make it happen. Don't be scared to fail, you'll be proud you tried.*

# THE BEST ADVICE I EVER GOT (WHETHER I LISTENED TO IT OR NOT)

> Work hard

> Enjoy it and have fun

> Call your parents every day

> Be nice to everyone – 'cause who you meet on the way up is who you'll meet on the way back down

> Be authentically you

> Learn to take criticism

> Not everyone will like you

> Put your money in a mortgage!

## The moment I realised what my biggest quality was

Arthur had a group called Magnetic Man, and asked me to be the singer on their tour back in 2012. I was a massive fan of dubstep (and Magnetic Man) growing up, so being asked to join them was a bit of a moment for me. I was starstruck, to be honest! We toured around the UK, playing in small sweaty venues, finishing one set at 3 a.m. and then driving through the night to play another set at 5 a.m. It was SO intense. But I loved it. Arthur looked after me and he's so hilarious, I just had the best time.

It was on that tour that I met the band Rudimental for the first time. After that tour finished, I went back into the studio to write some more songs and it was there one day I got an email saying that Rudimental were looking for a live singer for their tour, and would I like to audition? I thought, *F\*\*k it, why not?* But the audition day came around, and I had tonsillitis. GREAT! I turned up, and not only did I feel like s\*\*t, but there were two girls who'd already sung for them watching me from the doorway, plus it was the first time I had to put In-Ears in (these are the earpieces that you see singers wear when they're performing). I'd never used them before, and I found it massively distracting to have these things stuck in my ears while I was trying to concentrate on singing. I was like, *Rah, what the hell is this?*

It felt like the worst audition ever. I had no idea what was going on or what I was supposed to be hearing. I got really hot and angry, and their songs are really high so I got in a right state. I lost my s\*\*t. I was ill, I was pissed off and embarrassed, so I took my jacket off – which was tangled round my In-Ears – and I threw it at the wall. Rudimental were like, 'We love her! We wanna keep her!' And that was it. I got the job because I showed I had attitude. Hilarious.

*WorkLife Lesson: it's your own unique personality
that is your biggest asset. I thought I'd totally messed up the audition*

*by being so mardy, but they didn't see it like that – it was my honest reaction that they really loved. It was me being me, and that's so much better than putting on a front. So ask yourself and others what your best qualities are, and be proud of them.*

## The moment I realised all good things take time

It took SO long for me to make it. People think it happens overnight and once you're signed, boom, you're away – I mean, it took two years for me to even start writing my own music properly with Mary, and not just singing her songs! And even when I signed with my first management team they didn't know what to do with me. They'd take me to meetings with record companies, where I'd sing for a room full of people and not get a record deal!

Singing with Rudimental was going well though, and I learned so much from touring with them. It was exciting travelling the world, I was performing at gigs across the globe from Jamaica to Australia and everywhere in between – I even ended up performing at the O2 arena in London. Looking back, I didn't appreciate how huge that was. To be honest, it just felt stressful at the time, trying to sing every note right, hoping that I wouldn't get their lyrics wrong, that I looked good enough for them. Rather than appreciating what I'd achieved and giving myself a pat on the back, I was spinning out, worrying about everything that could go wrong. TYPICAL ME.

It was that gig, though, that led to me finally getting a record deal. But even then, it took ages to break through. I spent years in studios with different people, trying to write music (without knowing what I wanted to sound like, still). I released my first solo EP, *Karate*, in 2015, after three years of touring with the band, and even though it didn't go to number 1 in the charts, it got me the attention of bigger songwriters, like Steve Mac and

Ina Wroldsen. (Steve is a producer and songwriter who's co-written loads of massive hits like Little Mix's 'Woman Like Me', Ed Sheeran's 'Shape of You' and P!nk's "What About Us'. Ina is also an amazing songwriter who has co-written hits like 'Impossible' for James Arthur and 'Hold My Hand' for Jess Glynne.) It was with Steve and Ina that I wrote 'Alarm', which I released the next year. It was the first hit with my name on it and the song that changed everything for me – but it had taken years to get there.

> *WorkLife Lesson: if you want something, like, really*
> *REALLY want it, don't give up. Just don't. All those stories about*
> *'overnight successes' never show the full picture. You've just*
> *gotta keep going, even if you get knocked back a few times.*
> *Get back up! COME ON!*

## The moment I learned being yourself is enough

Back before I got a record deal, when I was still recording songs with Mary, my first manager asked me, in our first ever meeting, 'Who do you want to be?'. I was twenty years old, and that question totally floored me. I was like, *I have NO idea*. I mean, what? I didn't have a clue who *I* really was. Let alone what kinda artist I wanted to be. I'd spent so many years trying to get people to like me, bending my personality this way and that, I didn't understand what I was really about.

During this period I was hanging around with my new boyfriend at the time (let's call him Luke) and his bunch of university mates. I was faking it even then. I thought being around them was an opportunity to be somebody else, someone new, someone I wasn't. For example, I was collecting Jobseekers Allowance, but I pretended to them that I had loads of money. I pretended to be someone different to who I was. I faked *everything*.

I even thought I should change my name as an artist. I came up with some mad ideas – can you believe I thought I should be called 'Ruby Gold'? *F\*\*king hell.* And a few years later, when I got my first record deal, at twenty-four, I had to pretend then, too. Before the meeting, my ex-manager (yep, the same one) told me, 'Don't tell them you're from Essex, tell them you're from London. And don't wear a jumper from a charity shop, wear a dress instead.' He didn't want me to be myself, and I was like *For F\*\*K'S SAKE!* It was all a bit of a head wreck. I got the deal but it didn't feel as good as it could have done if I had got it being myself. It's like I had sold them a lie. I felt a fraud. When was the right time to be myself around them? Would I have to be this person forever? One day I might slip and say I'm from Essex. And would I be good enough when I finally showed my true self?

*Learning that I could be myself, and that it was OK to be me, took time.*

(Even on 'Alarm' I was told to sing it like Rihanna.) In fact, it wasn't until I met Ed Sheeran that I started to realise someone could just be themselves in the music industry. This was back in 2011, when I was introduced to him by my ex-manager, and it was crazy – he was in a room playing his new songs to Elton John, who was singing along! I was like, *WOOOOAAAHHH.* I couldn't believe it. After that, we met again properly in Paris, where he was doing a show and I was doing some writing. We got on really well, and from then on he was my biggest champion – telling his followers to follow me on social media, tagging me in posts, and eventually even asking me to go on tour with him, to open with my own set on his arena shows.

What I found so surprising about Ed, when we first met, was how authentic he is. He's just a lovely human, who happens to be one of the biggest artists in the world. And over time, he helped me realise it's totally fine to just be *yourself.* You don't have to pretend to be someone different to be special. That's what I used to think. But now, I'm myself; I'm honest and I'm the person I really am. What's crazy is that I discovered the more I was myself – my true self – in my career, the more successful I became. I faked who I was in that first meeting, I faked who I was for so long, and I've often wondered: what if I had been myself right from the start?

*WorkLife Lesson: you don't need to try to be someone*
*else to be special, or successful. I used to think being myself wasn't*
*good enough or would be boring and that I had to put on a fake front.*
*But it's rubbish. Being your authentic self is the*
*best thing you can be – and other people see that, too.*

## The moment when I realised outward success isn't everything

It was the morning after 'Rockabye' had been released in October 2016, and I woke up in my hotel room somewhere in middle America. My career was going absolutely crazy at this time – 'Alarm' had been released only a few months before, and I was finally starting to achieve the success that I'd been working all those years for. But I felt rubbish. I was working an insane schedule with my former manager, and I was totally destroyed. I looked like s**t and I felt like it too, I was absolutely exhausted and in a really bad place mentally. I turned over and checked my phone for the chart positions. 'Rockabye' was number 1 all over the world. I was like *Oh my god,* but I couldn't celebrate it properly. I was KNACKERED. It didn't feel like the moment of achievement it should have done, because I felt like s**t inside.

From the outside, I've had loads of success in my career but I never felt good about it until recently.

*All those years of striving, and I never felt really successful as a person.*

I think it was a combination of a few things: firstly, me not wanting to believe it was real in case it came crashing down tomorrow. Secondly, I had crazily high expectations of myself. Unless I was worldwide famous and every song was number 1, I didn't think I was successful enough (ridiculous, I know). Thirdly, and probably the most important reason, was because I felt s**t about myself.

It wasn't until I had therapy, and started to sort my head out, that I could begin feeling good about myself, and that included my career. It's said that self-improvement and success often go hand-in-hand, and that's how I think about it now. As I did more and more things with my music career, it felt good, don't get me wrong, but it didn't make me feel better inside. I'd have amazing experiences, and meet incredible people, like one girl who'd travelled from Brazil to the UK to see me perform, and another guy who'd got a tattoo of my signature on his chest. All this stuff blew my mind, but it didn't make me feel successful, because I had such low self-esteem. UGH.

Because I feel so differently about myself now, I can enjoy my career more. I think, *Wow, if I released 'Rockabye', 'Ciao Adios', 'Friends' and '2002' right now, I would be in my element!* I'd be like, *Rah, I am BRILLIANT!* But I didn't feel like me back then; there was always a crappy feeling inside me, even though the outside me looked successful. I didn't understand why I was like this until I had therapy. It's annoying, really, I wish I could have felt happy then, but better late than never! And it helped me understand success isn't about the shiny outward symbols we all think it is, it goes much deeper and more personal than that.

> *WorkLife lesson: career success means nothing*
> *unless you're happy with yourself, too. Don't sacrifice*
> *your personal happiness trying to chase a career goal,*
> *it won't mean anything when you get there.*

## The moment I understood what success really was

At the end of 2019, I was in LA and decided to go and see a couple of psychics. (I don't know whether they're for real or not, but I just love them!) They both told me separately, next year is gonna be your year, the year the universe aligns for you. I was all like, *Yessss, I feel everything is all going to make sense, I'm really happy with my new music, this is AMAZING.* I was really excited about everything and thought 2020 was going to be the career year to end them all. But then, obviously – COVID. The year ended up being nothing like I thought it was gonna be, and everything career-wise pretty much stopped. So what were the psychics chatting about?

Well, I went through 2020, came out of the other end and looking back now, I realise that they *weren't* talking about my career and they weren't talking about outward success, it was about what was going on inside me. They were saying that 2020 would be the year I found real success deep down – and they were right. I changed so much that year.

Really importantly, I learned to redefine success in my own way. Because I used to be someone who was constantly comparing myself to others' success, looking at the charts and seeking approval, asking people, *Am I doing OK? Am I successful?* I was always looking around and thinking I was crap compared with others.

*But it's all about shifting your perception of what success is and not measuring it by others' achievements.*

I realised what made me feel successful was making people happy with my music. Selling out venues, people taking their time to spend the evening with me for a show – that's what made me feel amazing. It means so much to me that people do that. Something that has always made me feel so good is when people tell me that a song of mine helped them get through something in their life. That's it for me – if someone tells me something like that I'm f\*\*king happy!

In 2021, I became a coach on *The Voice UK* – the singing talent show on ITV. When I was first approached about it, initially I was nervous and I wasn't sure, but my gut instinct told me, *Actually, this could be really great.* I had a Zoom call with the producers of the show (who were all female, which I loved), and I realised I was really passionate about becoming a coach, because I'd be able to talk about what it's like in the music industry right now, and also try to help contestants manage their mental health going through the process. I got a call a few days later, telling me they wanted me to be a coach; I was SO happy about it.

Filming the series during the lockdown of early 2021 was nerve-wracking, but I met the other coaches on set – Tom Jones, Olly Murs and will.i.am – and they were all so lovely to me, which put me at ease straight away. The whole way through the blind auditions stage – where the contestants sing to the coaches, but we can't see them because our chairs are turned around – I was so nervous, because I thought *No one is going to pick me to mentor them.* Once the first contestant picked me, though, I could relax and after that it was great! One amazing thing that I realised through doing this was how much I'd learned in my years in the music industry. The more it went on, the more worthy I felt of the whole experience. Being next to Tom and Will was incredible, too, I mean, that was a dream in itself!

That experience really helped me feel so confident in myself and my personality in a way I've not had before. I loved that people got to see who I was beyond just hearing my songs and got to know who I am. That was amazing for me, and the comments online throughout the series from fans, friends and family really solidified this. I've always wanted to be my authentic self, and now, people liking me for who I really am has made me go *F**k, wow! That's all I've EVER wanted!* That's what's really meaningful to me and has shifted my perception of 'success'. That I am successful, by being myself.

*WorkLife Lesson: other people's successes are not your failures – we are all on our own path. Find out what makes you feel successful inside and then strive to achieve that, not what society or social media tells you success is.*

# IF YOU'RE FEELING STRESSED ABOUT YOUR FUTURE . . .

Here are a few things that have helped me:

> You don't need to have a career plan all perfectly sorted – it's totally mad that people feel this expectation to know what they wanna do with their future at sixteen! Listen to the lyrics of one of my favourite songs, 'Everybody's Free (To Wear Sunscreen)' by Baz Luhrmann for some inspiration on this. This song has helped me a LOT.

> If you're stuck in a job or career you hate, you can change your mind and do something else – it's never too late. Life is short – make it count.

> If you're a decent person when you're trying to get ahead it counts for a lot. If I was a cock, there would be no way I would still be here. This industry is difficult, and being a nice person is important.

> Find some amazing mentors and supporters to champion you – there have been so many people, like Ed Sheeran, Annie Mac, Arthur, loads of music and media people who have helped my career because they wanted me to do well. You can't do it alone. I know it can feel hard sometimes to know where to start with finding a mentor, and it can feel quite scary asking for help and advice from someone. But actually, most people are REALLY flattered if you ask them. The best advice I can give is to look around at the people in your industry (or the industry you want

to get into), who are doing things you think are impressive, or who've had a career that you would love to emulate one day. Then get in touch with them, and – politely, of course – JUST ASK! The absolute worst that can happen is they don't reply, but they might very well reply and be chuffed to help. If you don't ask, you'll never know, so take the plunge.

> Don't be too proud to take positive criticism on board from people who know more than you. It might be hard to hear initially, but sit with it for a while and consider it from their point of view – which is what I had to hear from Arthur that time. If you start to think, *Huh, they might have a point*, then work on that and try to be grateful that you've received this advice.

> Perception can skew your view of success. If you're constantly comparing yourself to others you'll never feel successful. Success is individual, and you've got to forge your own path, rather than constantly trying to walk other people's. Remember, we can't all be Beyoncé!

## The ladder vs the iceberg

You know that phrase 'climbing the ladder'? It's the idea of how careers work; you start off at the bottom of a slope and gradually climb your way to the top, where you plant your flag and go, *Yay! I've made it!* And with a job like mine, where you're in the public eye, people can often assume that you've come out of nowhere – that one day you're trotting along as normal, and then the next you're a pop star and that it's all handed to you on a plate.

The way I see it, both of these ideas are complete bollocks.

As you can see, the journey I've been on has been waaay messier. What I've been through in my mad career path, and what I've learned, is that it's not like that at all. My road has been full of bumps, holes, twists, turns, a lot of luck, plenty of mistakes and even more hard work. And I've been helped along the way by some amazing people, who've given their time, support and advice to get me to where I am. And I owe them a lot.

But more than anything, I've learned a lot too. I've learned that we're all on different paths, we're all born to lead different lives, and what might be great for one person isn't for another.

*That there are loads of different ways to mark success.*

And that you don't actually climb a ladder *at all*. It's actually a bit more like an iceberg: other people only see the top 10 per cent of what you've done (the shiny outside bits), but underneath all that is the 90 per cent of work that you're doing behind the scenes!

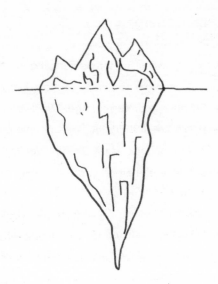

So whatever you want to do with your life, do it because YOU want to do it. Don't get caught up in living someone else's dream, or competing against someone else's achievements.

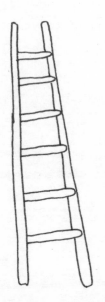

# IF YOU'RE FEELING UNMOTIVATED . . . TRY THIS

If you're feeling a bit 'meh', like you're lacking direction or motivation to keep going on your career path, try this exercise to set your week off on a positive note. On a Sunday night, sit down and think about your own unique qualities.

Ask yourself the question: what do I have?

Think about it and write down what they are below. Consider the qualities you have that belong to you as an individual and you only. (If you really can't think what they are, ask a good friend or family member):

*The qualities that make me, me*

................................................................................................................

................................................................................................................

................................................................................................................

................................................................................................................

................................................................................................................

................................................................................................................

................................................................................................................

................................................................................................................

................................................................................................................

Now, prepare for the week ahead. Write down what you want to achieve and tick it off as you go. Don't think of this as a boring to-do list, it's more like a list of small wins that you can do in the time frame possible. So obviously, it's not gonna be stuff like 'bag an amazing new job', because that's hard to achieve and you'll feel like crap if you don't do it. Maybe it's more stuff like 'arrange a coffee with XX', or 'update my online profile' or 'follow ten people in my industry on social media'.

*What I want to achieve*

..............................................................................................................

..............................................................................................................

..............................................................................................................

..............................................................................................................

..............................................................................................................

..............................................................................................................

..............................................................................................................

..............................................................................................................

..............................................................................................................

And remember: a new week always begins. A new day always begins. New goals, new achievements, new mindsets. Let's go!

No matter where I go, everybody stares at me / Not into fancy clothes, I'm rockin baggy jeans

# Discovering my true style, why it makes me happy and how to find yours

I recently found a picture of me from about ten years ago. I was just starting out as an artist, all dressed up for my first photoshoot. But I look COMPLETELY unrecognisable. Honestly, you wouldn't believe it was me. I struggled to believe it myself. I'm wearing some kind of gold corset bustier, a pointy shoulder shrug that goes up to my chin, and my hair is all gelled up in a quiff. My make-up is totally insane, too – I've got loads of black eyeliner on, some extra-long fake lashes and gold-coloured lipstick. It doesn't look like me at all. It's funny to think I even agreed to have photos taken looking like that.

I'm someone who's always wanted to dress differently, to not look the same as everyone else. And when I was a teenager, dressing exactly the way I wanted to, disregarding any trends or styles people were wearing at the time, was SO important to me. But I definitely struggled with that when I became an artist, and what I looked like became a massive issue for other people. Pictures like that one (and a few cringe others) definitely remind me of this!

I think how you dress is important, but not because it's about looking a certain way: sexy, fashionable, or whatever the latest trend is supposed to be. That's bollocks.

*How we style ourselves is our outward representation of who we are. It's us making a statement to the world, THIS IS ME.*

It's how we can convey a million and one things without even opening our mouths.

So what happened to me in that picture?

There are a lot of things that can affect us, I think. It can take a long time to find out who we really are and what our unique style really is, not least because everyone else has an opinion. And let's face it, there is a lot of pressure put on us around how we present ourselves to the world. We're sold unattainable 'perfect' images by adverts and the media, we listen to the opinions of people around us who don't matter, we try to make others happy by doing what they want, not what WE want to do.

I've made all these mistakes and loads more. Now I've finally got to a place where I feel like me, and I'm really happy with what I look like, but it definitely wasn't easy.

## Falling in love with style

I got really interested in clothes when I was a teenager. My dad was a Mod (this is a British fashion and music scene that dates back to the 1960s. People who are part of the Mod scene dress in a really distinct way – give it a google!) and dressed up sharp when we'd go out. He'd wear braces, shirt, a hat, tailored and stylish in the Mod style. We'd sometimes get up early on the weekend to go to Pitsea or Basildon market in Essex where we'd shop for bits and bobs. I also loved going to charity shops. It was so much fun.

Like most kids, when I was little I just followed the trends of the time. Me and my sister Sam loved flared jeans, anything sparkly and those massive belts that you wore around your hips. My fashion icons were singers like Gwen Stefani, P!nk and Christina Aguilera in the 'Can't Hold Us Down' video. Oh my god, I was OBSESSED with Christina – I loved her so much. I even told all my friends at primary school and my mum that I was going to change my name to Christina. My mum was not happy!

But that's what happens when you're younger, isn't it? You see someone who you think looks incredible – like Christina with her flat cap, low-rise jeans and super-thin eyebrows – and that's it, you wanna be EXACTLY like them. I'd do my best to copy her image, and as I hit my early teens, try to fit in with the crowd at school, who, as you know, were obsessed with brands, brands, brands.

## Faking it to fit in

I remember this one time, in secondary school, people were hanging out at the park. I tried so hard to cling on to the friendship group, I'd turn up uninvited! This particular time I was wearing a navy-blue velour tracksuit. It had the name on the waistband, and again it was not a cool, expensive brand so I was a bit embarrassed by it. I was so scared about people finding out what brand it was that I folded the waistband over so no one could see it. They asked, 'What brand is that?' I pretended, 'Oh, I don't know, I've got no idea.' I hate that now. I hate that I was embarrassed by that. I hate that they made me feel that way and I hate that I let them make me feel that way.

It's really sad, looking back now. I covered up the fact that I shopped at charity shops because it was considered uncool, even though it was something I really loved from such a young age. And it was natural for me to want to look different, but the peer pressure to fit in when I was young was so intense. It was all wrapped up in my desire to be liked – I thought if I wore the 'cool' stuff then they'd like me more. But it was a load of old bollocks really, and wasn't me at all. Now I couldn't care less about big brand names. I wear what I wanna wear, no matter where it is from!

## Unfollowing the herd

The thing was, my preferred style had always been a bit tomboyish, wearing jeans and trainers, steering away from dresses and skirts and heels. I loved putting random things together too, things that people wouldn't necessarily think would go.

As I got a little bit older, left school and went to college,

*I started not caring so much about what people thought and began to own my individual style more.*

It helped that the crowd I met at college had a completely different approach to brands than my school crowd – they were the complete opposite! If you wore a brand then it was like, 'Ugh, why are you wearing *that?*' It was uncool to be so mainstream, and seen as showing off. How confusing.

Being around these different attitudes meant I felt empowered to dress more openly in my second-hand clothes, and I became known as a proper individual dresser. I loved finding stuff that was a contrast to the norm and having a reputation as someone with a unique style. I loved and enjoyed wearing different clothes, and I wasn't scared about dressing in any way I liked. I even went through a period dressing like a Modette, a bit of a homage to my dad: I'd wear shirts, trousers, creepers (a kind of platform shoe) and cut my hair crazy as well, shaved at the sides and long at the back.

It's funny that it wasn't until I met people who perceived brands differently that I felt able to fully embrace my true, quirky, charity-shop-loving self. I was like, *Oh! I've been doing this FOREVER!* I thought I looked brilliant and it made me feel great that I could be completely myself with my clothes.

# HOW TO FEEL CONFIDENT IN YOUR CLOTHES

When you're growing up, it's tough sometimes to want to dress differently from your crowd. But just remember these few things:

> Trust your instincts: if you don't feel good in what you're wearing, don't wear it

> It is no one else's business what you wear: don't let anyone boss your style

> Some days you'll feel amazing but some days you'll feel like crap wearing the exact same thing. The way we feel about ourselves changes from day to day, whether we are bloated or hung-over or just a bit moody, and that's completely normal.

> What suits someone else won't always suit you: we're all built differently

> Personal style is a journey: you won't always get it right straight away, but that's part of the fun. Who would we be without a few embarrassing photos in our past, right?

## Standing out (while not wanting to stand out)

After college, I had a real obsession with not wanting to look the same as anyone else. That definitely came from always trying to look like other people at school. I'd felt so much pressure and worry to dress like the 'cool' crowd, in order to fit in, be liked and try not to get picked on. Once I got out of that school environment, I was so angry I had done that to myself that I was determined never to do it again.

I started to enjoy shopping in my own way again. I loved charity shops, because you'd pick up one-off pieces that were completely original, and you could be sure that nobody else would have the same as you. I'd actually go out to a bar or club with another outfit in my bag, just in case someone else was wearing the same thing! (a bit extreme I know!) I think that's where my obsession with two-pieces came from: it's easier to wear a top and bottom rather than a dress, because if someone's wearing the same top or bottom as me, that's only one thing I need to change in the toilets . . .

It's weird, isn't it, that I deliberately dressed in a way that made me stand out, when I was someone who didn't want to stand out because of my anxiety? This confused people. (And it confused me for a long time). When people would discover how self-conscious I was, they'd ask, 'Why do you look so different if you don't want people to look at you?'

It's a good question and to be honest, I only really figured this out recently, after speaking to Claire about it. I'd always known that I loved clothes and it was a really exciting way of expressing myself. But my experience at school made me push that side of me away. As I got older, I somewhat grew out of that. But I was subconsciously stuck with the worry of people looking at me from my time at school – and that's something I just couldn't budge. It was always bubbling underneath, even though on the outside you would never have guessed it.

*It was like a constant battle that went on inside me, between knowing I wanted to experiment with clothes and worrying about being judged for the clothes I loved wearing.*

*Ugh.*

## My image becomes everyone else's business

It was a huge shock when I first realised that what I wore and what I looked like was something for other people to get involved in. Obviously with most jobs, what you choose to wear and how you style your hair has got f**k all to do with your employer – as long as you look OK for the job you're doing, that's fine. But when I started taking my first steps into the music industry, I realised it was a huge thing that other people had VERY STRONG opinions about. GREAT.

It was hard for me to get my head around: clothes and hair were the two things that took me so long to enjoy for MYSELF and not anyone else. I had made a promise to myself to never care about what other people thought of my outfits or my hair anymore. But once I got into the industry they were the things people started telling me I needed to change.

Going to my first meetings with people in the music industry when I was twenty, I was told to dress 'more funky glam and less sporty – no jeans, no trainers'. I was told not to wear my beloved charity shop jumpers, and that I needed to 'try to look a bit more like an artist' instead. I mean, what the hell? I got sent out on a shopping trip with an assistant from the management company to get more glamorous stuff. It was fun, because they let me go to a vintage store (I at least insisted on that), but it still wasn't the stuff I would have chosen to wear myself. It was more obviously 'sexy' stuff – a red mini dress, a black mesh t-shirt dress, which was see-through to the bra and knickers underneath. (ARGH.)

I'd get emails before meetings reminding me, 'You need to look amazing. I would advise wearing heavier eyeliner and your red lipstick' and 'just look like a star'. I would look around at other female artists who were coming out on the scene around the same time and think, *Oh f\*\*k – I've got to look like them*. They looked absolutely amazing, really sexy and glamorous, but I knew it wouldn't be right for me. But I did it. I thought this is what I have to look like to be a female artist and be popular. Hence that photo I told you about at the start.

It was so hard to have this fight with people when you're trying to make it – and also when you don't know exactly who you are yet, which I didn't. I was still young, and still wanted everyone to like me. I didn't want to get a reputation as a difficult person to work with and so my teenage insecurities came back to say hello. Although I knew I liked dressing differently, because I was so worried about people not liking me and mugging me off behind my back, I just did what they wanted. The one thing I promised myself to never care about again went right out the f\*\*king window. It was a really tough time. I knew what they wanted to style me in wasn't right, but I was in that place where I thought they probably knew better than me, too. So I gave in.

I did try, though. One time I sent an email to try to explain the sort of image I wanted to have. 'I saw this girl today and like her style, with loads of necklaces! Leather jacket, Nike Air Force 1s,' I wrote. Their reply? A shutting-me-down 'Hmmm. I like elements of it, but not everything.' *Annoying.*

# BEING THE ONE WITH CRAZY HAIR (AND WHY I LOVED IT)

I've always experimented with my hair. I think it came from that time in my early teens when I was getting grief for my clothing choices. I'd think, *Right, I'll give them something to talk about.* So I started doing mad s\*\*t with my hair (which is naturally a light brown colour), colouring it all kinds of crazy ways so that people would look at that rather than what I was wearing. The first thing I did was put blonde and red highlight stripes in – it was disgusting, really, but I loved it because it was a bit rebellious, too. You weren't allowed to dye your hair at our school, and so I got in trouble. I loved it.

Once I got to college, I met a hair colourist who needed models to test out different colours on. It was perfect for me, because firstly, I was able to change my hair all the time, and secondly, I could do it without spending any money! Win-win. From then on I was known as the one with crazy hair, which suited me fine.

I'd always had the approach that if you don't like your hair, you can cut it or dye it. No big deal. Other people around me saw their hair as really precious and that's not something I'd ever felt. I loved the feeling that I could change it at a moment's notice, and when I started singing with Rudimental, that's exactly what I did. I went through all different colours – peach, brown, purple, pink – and wild haircuts, from really short to plaits and everything experimental. It was so much fun.

But as soon as I became a solo singer, my label told me, 'You've got to keep it blonde and you've got to keep it the same length.' Their reasoning was that they needed people to recognise me and if I kept changing my hair, they wouldn't. I felt like, *This is the worst thing anyone could ever say to me, because my hair is my freedom!* It was really hard – throughout the '2002' and 'Friends' time I kept it the same, although I was desperate to shave it and dye it all different colours.

After I finished promoting the *Speak Your Mind* album, I wanted to change my hair colour for each song I released after that. That was a solid NO. Right, I thought, I'll pick just one hair colour then – pink. Pink is gonna be the new hair colour for me! And I came up with a cunning plan. I thought, I'll write about it in my songs, which I did in 'Birthday' ('Told my friends to come over /To dye my hair') and 'To Be Young' ('Dye my hair a million colours/Dream I'll make a billion dollars') so they can't tell me I'm not allowed. To be honest, I really like my hair pink – it's a great colour. But if it was up to me, I'd have a different hair colour every week.

So if you're able to – embrace your hair freedom. Experiment with new cuts and colours. Chop it off, even if it is just a little – it'll grow back. Put a semi-permanent shade in – it'll wash out. Doing something new with your hair is so exciting, and made me feel so free. Crazy-hair Anne-Marie will be back one day!

## Finding the way towards my authentic image

The more my career progressed, the more I started to assert myself a bit more with my clothes and style. A lot of it was through a simple process of elimination: working out what worked, and what didn't. Firstly, I realised I can't perform in heels – so they went out the window, *Bye-bye, see ya, ciao adios* (did I really just quote my own song?). Then another time when I was performing, I sat at the edge of the stage, got up, and my bum was on full view for the crowd. Someone filmed it and I watched it back. The beauty of the Internet, huh? (Please don't go and find that video now haha.) *Right,* I thought, *I'm never wearing a f\*\*king skirt again* . . . I started to filter down the sorts of clothes I would wear bit by bit.

When I was just being myself, rather than performing and singing, I had no stress deciding what I wanted to wear. For example, I'd always worn sliders with socks from when I was about eighteen (Claire used to take the piss out of me for that). It had always been my thing. But that style that I wanted to wear as an artist, oversized jumper, socks and sandals, was never accepted by the people from my first management team. It was a big no for them.

I kept trying to tell stylists what I wanted to wear, but it was hard. It would always be a bit of a fight, which would really confuse me. I'd be like, *Why can't you just let me wear what makes me happy? I'm the person who's dressing in this!* But I'd often be in a room full of people telling me, 'Oh, you look AMAZING,' even when I said I didn't like it. I'd end up convincing myself that wearing their outfit choice was the right thing to do. I'd stop believing my own instincts, go along with it and wear the outfit that I didn't feel like myself in. UGH. It's honestly SO ANNOYING even writing this. I wish I had just been more of a stubborn bitch!

*It took years to get to the point where I learned how to say NO.*

I realised my style is my thing and I'm going to make the most of it. I started working with a different stylist, one who really 'got' me, rather than ones where our conversations would go something like this:

*Me: I just want to wear two-pieces that match, both oversized, with socks and sliders, and loads of jewellery and sunglasses.*
*Stylist: Ohhhh . . . right, yeah, I like that. I also think you would look amazing in this dress and heels to show off your body a bit more.*
*Me: ARGGGHHHHH*

For so long, I felt that what I wanted to wear that was true to me – my baggy, tomboyish, charity-shop style – wasn't good enough for what I was 'meant' to look like as a female pop star. But I eventually got there, and now the stuff I wear is totally right for me. I feel confident and completely myself.

## THE OUTFITS I FEEL MOST KICK-ASS IN

> A tracksuit

> A tracksuit

> A tracksuit

> A tracksuit

> Erm . . . another tracksuit?

## Learning what suits my body

*One of the biggest points about style that I've learned over the years is knowing what suits ME and my body shape instead of trying to copy other people.*

Just like all of us, I've been guilty of being influenced by images when I'm online shopping – you know, when you see a model looking f**king brilliant in something, so you buy it, but then when it arrives and you try it on, you look like a sack of potatoes? It took me AGES to learn that when this happened, it wasn't my problem, I just had a different body shape to the models I was seeing. What looked good on them didn't necessarily look good on me (and vice versa). And THAT IS FINE.

We are all different body shapes, and if this was a completely accurate representation, there'd be almost eight billion different drawings here. Every SINGLE ONE of our bodies is different to any other. We might sway more towards a certain category, but there is no way we'd find a picture of someone with exactly OUR body, because no one else has our body, except us! (And on that note, someone pointed out on social media recently that even if we ALL ate the same diet and did the same workouts, we'd still look completely different. So there you go).

As soon as I started working all this stuff out, I was able to start making my wardrobe work for me. I'll give you an example – I realised a while ago that I suit high-waisted trousers. Once I got that in my head, I started asking stylists not to bring trousers that sit below the waist to photoshoots, and I stopped buying ones like that for myself at home. It was a gradual process of editing and removing certain styles that didn't suit me. Eventually I got to the place I am now, where I don't have any trousers in my wardrobe that don't suit me – because they're ALL high-waisted. *Bingo!*

I used to think things didn't suit me because there was something wrong with my body. But that's crap. It was a long process to filter this negative self-talk out, and figure out that it is FINE for things not to suit me when they suit someone else. By knowing what doesn't suit you you're able to work out what DOES suit you instead. And there's no rush to it, you can just work it out as you go along.

# THE STYLES THAT SUIT ME

**Trousers:** High-waisted ones, above the belly button, please

**Tops:** Baggy, baggy, baggy t-shirts

**Neckline:** square cut, off the shoulder

**Dresses:** If I ever wear a dress, I need one that pulls me in at the waist. I don't suit dresses that go straight down, or are loose at the waist

**Skirt:** It has to be a mini length, ending halfway down my thigh. If it goes past this, it looks totally weird on me.

**Shoes:** Always sliders. And if I ever need to wear heels, they have to be a platform and have a strap going around above my ankle, because it makes my legs look nicer.

**Jewellery:** big, chunky and gold

# THE STYLES THAT SUIT YOU

Trousers:

........................................................................................................

Tops:

........................................................................................................

Neckline:

........................................................................................................

Dresses:

........................................................................................................

Skirt:

........................................................................................................

Shoes:

........................................................................................................

Jewellery:

........................................................................................................

## Dressing a bit more sexy (because I want to)

As you know, I generally enjoy dressing a bit more like a tomboy. It just so happens that those sorts of clothes are the ones that I feel best and most comfortable in. But I think in the back of my head, I did have a bit of an issue with being seen as 'sexy' with what I wore. I didn't want anyone to look at me in that way.

I didn't want to be seen as an object, I wanted people to see me as just another person. That attitude definitely fed into the sorts of clothes I chose to wear, and that's OK, but it was a negative approach. Although I wore what I liked, there was definitely an element of covering up going on, too.

*I didn't want people looking at my body, because I didn't feel good about it.*

When I was young, I used to love singers like Britney and Christina but I would never dress like them as an artist. I loved P!nk's style because I could relate to her look – she was a tomboy, but she was also sexy and powerful. She actually really helped me as an artist; I could see, thanks to her, that I COULD be a female singer and not have to dress a certain way. Although I had to fight my own battles, knowing that singers like her, Adele and Avril Lavigne bucked the norms of what female artists were expected to look like gave me confidence.

Over time, I've become WAY happier with my body, and that started to feed into slightly changing up the sorts of clothes I'll wear. I started to feel more comfortable with wearing 'sexier' clothes every now and then, and I'll be honest, I also had the thought of, *Well, I'm not going to look like this forever, so I may as well f\*\*king show it off now!*

187

It was a lovely feeling to have because I was embracing my body and showing it off – on my terms – not because I wanted to people please. I make those decisions now for myself. So, if I suddenly think, oh, I want to be a bit more sexy tomorrow, and wear a short skirt or something, that's OK. I want to wear it because *I want to*. It helps that I care a lot less, if at all, about what people think of my appearance now. So I'm not holding myself back anymore. Also, someone will ALWAYS have something to say about what you're wearing. When I wear a tracksuit people say, 'Have you just rolled out of bed?' but when I wear something with more skin showing, some people say that I should cover up. You will *never* win if you are dressing for other people's approval. There is no point, so wear whatever you want to wear.

Of course, if you don't feel ready to be sexy, then that's OK too. I'd never EVER want to tell you what to do with your body and your clothes, and nobody should for that matter! I'm just happy that I've come to a place where I feel comfortable dressing sexy every now and then. And if you are too, then that's great. And if you never wanna dress sexy then that is great too. YOU DO YOU. I just want you to be completely authentic about the way you dress – that you're wearing what YOU want to, to make YOU happy, not someone else . . .

## Making up with make-up

Nobody should ever say to someone that they shouldn't or can't wear make-up.

*If you wanna wear make-up, wear it – and I repeat, if YOU want to.*

Make-up is like art; many make-up artists I know study make-up tutorials and get really into the self-expression side of it. That side of make-up is amazing, because it allows you to create infinite different looks and is really creative.

The problem with make-up is when you do it because you don't feel good about yourself. Obviously, it's fine if you feel like you want to cover up a few spots, or try to make your eyelashes a bit longer, but I think a lot of us are really negatively affected by filters (I mean that's a whole different story right there).

*We've been so negatively influenced by this cult of perfection, a lot of us have lost perspective of what's normal.*

These apps and magazines make people look so smooth and spotless, but literally NO ONE can look like that in real life. It's not possible. But it's understandable if that's all you see, you can start to develop a warped idea of what you should look like. People become scared to look like themselves.

I know this because it's how I used to feel. I used make-up to hide my

189

face because I didn't like it. I used it to make people look at something else, not my natural features. I used to wear really thick black eyeliner for that reason. And when I was in Rudimental, my friends had a running joke that everyone was constantly waiting for me to do my eyebrows. Eyebrows and eyeliner were my two 'things' – I'd spend ages piling on loads and loads of make-up so that people would be distracted by it, instead of looking at my actual face.

Eventually, I thought, *This is so long and stressful, I need to learn to love my face without make-up.* It took time but I started to change my mindset, and wear less and less make-up. I still wear make-up now. I LOVE make-up! I love that lipstick can be like an accessory to your outfit, like a pair of sunglasses or shoes. But I don't feel I have to plaster it on to feel beautiful anymore. Now, I'm finally as comfortable with make-up on or off – sometimes feeling my best, sometimes feeling my worst. But I've got to be honest, it wasn't an overnight process. It took me a long time to really like my face without the protective layer of make-up.

So wear make-up, or don't wear make-up, whatever. It's your decision. But I don't ever want you to feel like you NEED it – 'cause you don't.

*Your face is amazing – it is unique and different to everyone else's.*

People have pimples and birthmarks and scars – everyone. And that is exquisite. I want you to be proud of your beautiful, unique face, with or without make-up.

# 10 BEST INSTAGRAM MAKE-UP ACCOUNTS FOR INSPIRATION

@sirjohn

@nikki_makeup

@nyxcosmetics_uk

@monaleannemakeup

@lady0pal

@kickiyangz

@babenexttdoor

@laurelcharleston

@mimles

@rowisingh

# IF YOU'RE FEELING UNCONFIDENT . . . KNOW THIS!

A big part of style is completely inexplicable, because it's really about something you can't see, or touch: *the way you feel inside.* When you feel like yourself in an outfit, it's the best feeling ever. When you don't feel like yourself, it's poop.

So if you're feeling unconfident about the way you look, really ask yourself: why do I feel like this? Is it an itchy top that you don't really like? Or trousers that hang a bit weird? Or the colour of your dress you're not sure about? Be honest with yourself about how your clothes make you feel, and get rid of the elements that make you feel like crap. Leave the house every day, 100 per cent confident in the outfit you're wearing. Make sure you are comfortable.

Because I promise you, how you feel is key to finding more confidence in your clothes. It affects EVERYTHING. When I wasn't happy with outfits and went on stage or just walking out the door doing everyday, normal things, I'd be really worried about what other people were thinking about them. It was very distracting when I was trying to give people the best show I could. It was always unnecessary agg when I didn't feel like 'me' in an outfit, and it was what I was trying to tell people for so long.

My tour manager is one of the best humans I know: he's amazing because he tells me literally everything, which I love. We have conversations about styling a lot and he once told me, 'I just want to let you know, when I look at your Instagram I can tell when you've styled yourself – you look much better.' And I was like, 'Yep.' That's

> it for me — I know that now. It's taken me years to build that confidence in myself. And you can too.

## The key to owning your own style . . .

. . . is caring less about what other people think.

Simple, right? NO. I know I can tell people this over and over again, and it still won't go in. I know because I was the same; I used to read this in quotes all the time, and it didn't make a blind bit of difference until, suddenly, it did. One day, it clicked in my head and I went, *Oh yeah*. I know you need to work it out for yourself, but I'll keep banging on about it to help you get there.

*The great thing about worrying less about what people think of you is that it gives you freedom. You take that worry away and your life is yours.*

You decide whatever you want because you want to, rather than making decisions based on what other people think. That's the biggest thing I've learned.

So try to tune into what you love. You might wear similar clothes to your friends, but add a bit of your own unique thing – maybe that's massive earrings, knee-high socks or a different hairstyle – make sure there's always something that's really *you*. Doing this and ENJOYING IT will do your confidence wonders, too.

You are a different human being to everyone else. So make the most of it. You know what you like deep down. Be the leader of your own style: just do whatever you feel like. Don't think about what other people are wearing. Or what their hair looks like. You wanna do something else – go for it!

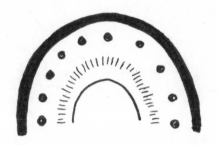

Ain't no time to play pretend / What you see is what you get

# Living my online life, authenticity, and how I learned to have a healthy relationship with social media

t was 2014, I was touring with Rudimental and I had cut my hair really short. I *loved it*, and thought it really suited me. All my friends had said how amazing it looked, too, so I decided to post a picture of my new hair on Instagram. I had more followers these days than before, because a lot of Rudimental's fans had started following me. But it hadn't changed how I treated my social profile, I was just carrying on as I always had, putting the same stuff online that I'd done when it was only my friends and family following me. But I had no idea how much things had already changed for me on social media.

Really hyped, I posted the picture and forgot about it for a few hours. But later that night I was at Claire's house and started flicking through the comments. Most were nice, but there were quite a few from people who hated my new hairstyle, and thought I should know about it. 'What have you done?!' said one. 'Grow your hair back,' said another. 'You look like a boy' was another one. I couldn't believe it, it felt like a punch to the stomach. Why would people be horrible? I cried a lot and felt totally gutted because I had thought my hair looked great. Even though I didn't know who the people were that were commenting, it was devastating to read how bad they thought I looked.

> *That was a real turning point for me. I realised from then on that my life online had changed.*

I now couldn't do *anything* without other people having an opinion about it, and believing it was their divine right to share that opinion with me. Initially, it made me feel really sad. I wasn't used to this kind of direct criticism — after all, I was massively insecure and sensitive, as you already know! And as soon as I read those negative comments, it made me doubt my new hair. It changed quickly just because of the words of a few strangers.

At Claire's that night, she did her best to make me feel better. 'Some people are always going to have a negative opinion, and you've just got to build up a hard wall,' she said. She was right: people were now going to start saying whatever they wanted about me online, and there was nothing I could do to change that. I decided that I was going to build up that wall.

First of all, I tried to brush the bad comments off. Whenever people would post something negative about me, I'd screenshot it and send it to my friends as a sort of joke. I'd claim that it didn't bother me (it did), and I was just showing them for a laugh (which it really wasn't). In those moments, my friends would comfort me, send me nice comments, and hug me if they were there with me. But when I was on my own, it was really hard to cope with the horrible stuff people would post, because I *believed* what they were saying.

## Obsessing about the comments

Although I was developing a hard shell on the outside, inside I was still really affected by what people would post about me online. Early on in my career, I would google myself all the time. I'd read every single comment on Instagram and YouTube about me. My friends would tell me to stop looking, but it was so hard! It's natural to want to know everything that people say about you – and I was obsessed. Yuk.

It was especially hard if you were like I was, where you wanted *everyone* to like you. It was like a sort of self-harm: I knew it was gonna happen, that there would always be someone putting something s\*\*t out there, but I couldn't stop myself from searching for it. It's so true that you read ten good comments and there's one half bad one and that's the one you latch on to.

(There's that negativity bias again, I hate our brains sometimes. Actually, on that note, wouldn't it be AMAZING if our brains just remembered the positive things people said about us? We'd be walking down the road and just reminiscing happily about the lovely things people have said about us, like, *Oh yeah, remember that time when someone commented that I looked incredible? I am just fantastic.* But that never happens!)

When I posted stuff I was really happy with and I'd see a bad comment it would really f\*\*k me up. I'd think, *Yes, that's how I feel about myself, that is correct.* I'd totally believe they – the anonymous troll – were right and I'd probably delete the photo straight away. How mad is that? But when you're in a bad place and you feel low, you search for it to confirm how you feel about yourself. It's a cycle. You get stuck in the feedback loop of hell . . .

## FEEDBACK LOOP OF HELL

feel like
s..t

search for
negativity

believe it

find
negativity

### Feelings aren't facts

Thank god I don't do that anymore. The older I've got and since I started therapy and feeling better in myself, I've cared less about what other people think – and that's especially true about people who don't know me personally. It's just too much effort to worry about! It's one of my favourite things about getting older actually, not having to care as much. I still read comments as I am online a lot, but I don't go searching for the *negative* stuff.

*I also started to realise that what people said wasn't actually true, it was an opinion, not a fact.*

I mean, thinking about it, it's actually pretty obvious, but it's so easy to forget this when you're caught up in the comments posted on social media – you believe in everything negative that other people say. One incident that really brought this home for me was when I saw two completely opposing comments on the same picture of me. One person had posted, 'she's looking chubby', whereas another had said, 'she's lost weight'. I mean, *HA!* It made me sit up and think, hang on a minute, that can't be right, can it? How can I possibly believe one of them when they're saying completely different things about the same photo?

Becoming more aware of our mental health, and how we are ALL dealing with it every day, has also helped me get distance from what people post online. It's easy to be anonymous and hide behind a fake online profile, and I know that the people who are posting s**t online actually have things going on themselves. They're not happy people who are somehow more knowledgeable than me – they're actually hurting deep inside themselves. They're just pushing out the hate they feel and putting it onto other people, even if they don't realise it. And that actually makes me feel sad and want to cuddle them. (Imagine that, wanting to cuddle people that are calling you fat. Hahaha.)

It's that mentality of having to post all your thoughts online that I still have trouble with, though. Like, not necessarily nice comments, but the nasty ones, I mean, *why do you have to do it?* Literally, why do you have to think something negative and then type it? Why do you feel that your horrible opinion needs to be seen by everyone? I don't get it. And YES it is fine to have an opinion about someone, but you REALLY don't have to post it on social media. Especially if it's mugging someone off.

## Don't feed the troll

Not only did I have to wake up to the fact that people were gonna have an opinion on ME and not like everything I do (R.I.P. that kick-ass haircut), but I also had to come to terms with the fact that I couldn't put out my gut reactions on social media, either.

This all came to a head once when I reacted in the heat of the moment to a post on social media years ago. A woman had commented negatively on Rudimental's latest video, saying it was 'anti-white' because it was set in a barbershop. I thought this was just ridiculous, so I posted back, 'God, I wish I could punch you through the screen!' What I didn't know was that she was pregnant. FFS. Everyone piled onto me, like, 'Oh my god, Anne-Marie, how could you punch a pregnant woman!'

I mean, *give me a break,* of course I didn't know that before I posted. But that moment taught me that social media was different, and putting it out there meant it had an overwhelming response it never would have had in reality. You can't understand the context from a few written words. You can't hear the tone of voice used. You can't see the expression on someone's face when they type it: I realised that it's not just my little thoughts now – people are actually paying attention. That's when it hit me; s\*\*t, I can't say what I say in real life on social media.

I was pissed off about this at the time, because I wanted to be outspoken about the things I feel strongly about. I felt like I'd been silenced. Back then, I was still quite an angry person, and I wanted to be able to be opinionated about everything. But I slowly accepted that it didn't go down well to be like this online. It wasn't always the right place, and it was harder to get subtleties across (or jokes, haha), because people were always going to take it any way they pleased, no matter what my intentions actually were.

I learned something important though, which was:

*you don't have to react in the moment on social media. In fact, it's better not to.*

I read something brilliant about this, which was 'Don't react when you're angry, and don't reply when you're sad.' I completely agree. Nowadays, I can read something, and yes, I might *think, What a f\*\*king prick, what do they think they're playing at?* but I don't have to post it. I can just send a screenshot to my friends, have a moan and then I'll get over it. In the end, it's very rare that I post anything angry or reactive at all anymore. Because why do I have to vomit up all my thoughts online?

# FIVE QUESTIONS TO ASK YOURSELF BEFORE YOU POST THAT COMMENT . . .

> Are you angry or pissed off? If so, take a few minutes to calm down and consider why you want to put this emotion out there.

> Are you posting something negative? If so, why? I mean SERIOUSLY – WHY? Let me tell you something, being horrible to someone online NEVER makes you feel better

> Would you say this comment to a friend? To their face? Really, would you? And they wouldn't punch you for it?

> How would you feel if someone said this to you? Really happy and grateful? Or actually, would you feel really hurt and find it hard to let go of that comment?

> Are you posting about someone famous? Remember: they might read it and feel crap. They're a human being, just like you, and they have feelings, too.

## Back in the day

When I was a teenager, there wasn't really social media in the same way there is now. Instead, we spent hours texting, and on MSN and MySpace. I *loved* MySpace when it first came along. In the mid 2000s, MySpace was the biggest social media site out there, and was huge all around the world. It was the first site you went on where you could connect with all your friends, personalise your own backgrounds and set the theme. It was fun to give your online self a personality: it felt exciting that people would know what I was like and what I was into just by looking at my profile. Ahhh, innocent days . . .

When MySpace introduced their Top Friends feature, though, it really pissed me off. It was a section on your page where you would choose your top eight friends, and it was *savage*. Looking at other people's Top Friends, I'd constantly worry and wonder if I was on anyone's and feel sad if I wasn't. It was the first time the Internet felt personal to me. Before that, the online world felt like something completely separate. It was somewhere I would go to look for stuff, but it wasn't anything to do with me, as there was no 'me' online. But this was the start of it all.

But there were good elements to growing up, then, too – especially because we weren't addicted to our phones. Of course, I remember having phones all the way through my teen years – and especially being really proud of my Nokia 3310. (I was always that person who wanted the newest, best phone around, ha!) But the difference back then was that they weren't smartphones – you couldn't use the Internet on them, there weren't such things as apps, and social media was still a really new thing that you couldn't access on your phones. So, our phones were there for texting and calling and playing Snake and that was pretty much it. I remember going out and not even looking at it once. Shocking, I know! Often, I still crave that feeling of going out to the pub with a group of mates, without everyone being on their phones all the time. But I do feel like my friends and I are more aware of that now and try to keep our phones away when we spend time together.

## Why social media is changing the world for the better

There are so many incredible things social media has done for us, and I think we should celebrate that. Too often, the media (and us!) get so caught up in focusing on the negativity around it, we forget about all the amazing things that it has allowed us to do. I believe it's changing the world for the better, and the good parts MASSIVELY outweigh the bad.

### *Social activism:*
Social media has given people a voice who didn't have a voice before, and it's helping mobilise the world to change. If you look at movements like Black Lives Matter and #MeToo, I personally think they wouldn't have had as much attention or impact without the power of social media. We can connect with each other across the globe, spread awareness of issues that don't get covered elsewhere and even post video evidence about things that matter. I think it's changing our moral compass for the better.

It's amazing to be exposed to movements and stories online like BLM, but what's really important about these sorts of issues is to carry on their changes in real life. It's not enough just to do stuff online – to like a few posts or post a comment offering support – we have to engage in real life to make real changes. I've always worked hard to make sure the teams I work with and the music videos I make are diverse and representative. Racism is also something I will NEVER shy away from speaking up about on social media and in real life. There is not another side of the argument when it comes to racism, it is just wrong.

In summer 2020, I went down to take part in the Black Lives Matter protest in London. It was an incredible experience. Being surrounded by thousands of other people who feel just as strongly as you do, where you're all united on a single cause, felt so empowering. It made me feel really emotional too – as you'll see from the video below. Protests have been ongoing for generations, and they've often incited positive changes around the world, so it was such a great thing to be a small part of.

### Body positivity:

When I was younger, all I cared about was being skinny and having a boyfriend, and that definitely wasn't made any better by all the non-diverse images I saw in magazines – thin, white models. There weren't even many larger-sized clothes in the shops! It wasn't a very inclusive environment, and gave me a really narrow definition of what female bodies should look like.

I know Instagram has a lot to answer for when it comes to unattainable body images, but they didn't invent that. And what you see now is loads more people posting body shots with no filters. People have become so much more aware of the power of honesty, and they'll put pictures up of their stretchmarks, their belly rolls and their acne. I didn't used to know there was stuff like this up there, but I remember coming across someone posting honest pics of her belly a while ago, and I thought, *That's so f\*\*king cool!* It really helped me. Having images like this up is such a positive thing overall, helping everyone to see that perfection is a myth, and we should accept every body shape and size.

# 10 BEST BODY POSITIVE ACCOUNTS ON INSTAGRAM

@charlihoward                @chessiekingg

@stephanieyeboah            @celestebarber

@harnaamkaur                @bryonygordon

@iamlshauntay               @theslumflower

@ariesmoross                @i_weigh

*Mental health:*

Don't get me wrong, we've got a long way to go still, but social media has helped start to de-stigmatise mental health a hell of a lot. Beforehand, if you were feeling depressed or anxious, you would have struggled to find someone going through the same thing you were. Unless there was someone you knew in your immediate social circle who was also having a bad time, how would you feel able to speak about it? But now, mental health groups and general people online and on social media have done wonders for helping us — you can connect with people and organisations who understand, support and help you get through.

There's also been a massive change in how chatting about mental health is perceived. People who were struggling would have felt negatively judged if they admitted how they really felt, because the media coverage about mental health back in the day was so unsupportive and not understanding. Now, thanks to the thousands of people that speak openly about their mental health challenges, it's become way less stigmatised than before, which is great. The more people that talk about it, the less shame is attached to it, and I think social media is to thank for this.

### *Education:*

I've learned more on social media than I EVER learned at school! Honestly, I didn't know anything about the world when I was younger – I didn't know what the f**king map looked like, or where anything was, I was oblivious to anything outside my little bubble. But through reading articles and watching reports I've been alerted to by others on social platforms, I've learned so much more about important issues and news around the world from my own research online. I've connected with different communities and different people, read about history, geography and politics. Things that I never knew about before, and wouldn't have known about if it hadn't been for social media. It's opened my mind.

I'm really excited about the future, because people now are so much more educated about everything, thanks to social media. They don't just accept what's written in the bulls**t papers and take that as their own opinion without challenging anything. They search for themselves to find out what's going on in the world, and take action. That makes me so happy. I feel like the younger generation is gonna change the world.

## How we can combat the negativity online

If we all used social media in the right way it would be the most beautiful thing ever. But obviously it's not like that, and for a lot of us, it can be a place that fuels our anxieties. I'm the same as everyone else, really, and

I've had crap times on social media. I get that it can be a really hard place for a lot of people.

### Rewarding the extreme:

One thing that worries me is that I feel like social media has made everyone think you have to be extreme. People can feel that in order to be noticed, you need to do something dramatic or have experienced something extreme. Not that these things don't go on, but because the dramatic stuff gets a lot of likes and attention, for a lot of people, they feel that being ordinary isn't enough. Because if you're 'normal' you're swept under the rug, and no one pays attention to you.

### Making us feel we're not enough:

It's easy to forget that so much of what we see on social media is about making us feel that we lack something. Lack is what fuels our consumerist society – advertisers and companies make us feel that if we only had this flawless skin and this glossy hair and bought this amazing product, we would feel better. But none of this is true – it's all created.

Think about it – when was the last time that you bought a product to make your hair glossy and then actually thought, *Brilliant, I'm completely happy and satisfied with who I am now!* I bet NEVER, because it doesn't work! They create issues out of things we don't actually have an issue with – because in reality, we as individuals don't actually lack anything. Sure, we can work out and eat healthily for our own body and brain's sake. But we don't actually NEED any of this stuff. We are enough as we are.

### Bringing out our negative side:

Social media can bring out our worst tendencies too – just look at the clickbait headlines to see what I mean. Those crappy links are never about 'look at this lovely person', they're usually 'oooh, look how bad this person looks now'. It's playing on that negativity bias we all have again: we want other people to feel or look s**t because we do about ourselves. But just chasing the negative never makes us feel better about ourselves.

### Feeding trolls and haters:

And of course, there are Internet trolls. As someone in the public eye, I've been really lucky overall, because people have been really kind to me across social media in comparison to a lot of other – in particular – female artists in the industry. People can be vicious about some others, and I've often wondered, how do you mentally cope with it when everyone is turning the hate on? I'm so lucky that I've got the people following me that I do. If there's EVER anything bad out there about me, my fans protect me more than I protect myself! That's the only reason I'm still OK with it, but if I was getting cussed all the time, I wouldn't be online, ever.

Even with my negative experiences, which haven't been that bad, it's hard not to listen to trolls if they're confirming what you feel about yourself. It wasn't until I was happier in myself that I was able to remove myself from negative comments. A few years ago, if I posted a picture and someone commented that I looked fat, I'd take that on. Now, because I love myself, those things don't affect me in the same way. If someone said to me now, 'Your hair is crap,' I'd be like, *Hahahahaha you're funny! No it's not, it's actually brilliant. Do one!*

# IF YOU'RE FEELING INSECURE . . . MY MANIFESTO FOR A HEALTHIER FUTURE ON SOCIAL MEDIA

Social media would be so much better for all of us if we could get rid of the worst parts of it, and change it up. Here are my ideas for how we can make it a happier place that makes us all feel better in ourselves:

### Natural Honesty, Not Toxic Positivity

Social media is hard because you can be whatever you think you *should* be, and so even if you're feeling sad you can pretend to be happy. It's that tendency towards toxic positivity that doesn't help ANYONE, so rather than only presenting the pretty, curated, 'best bits' of our lives, let's stop pretending everything is awesome. Instead, let's be honest about the messy parts of life – because we all know that sometimes things are great, sometimes they're not. If you've got a baby, don't just post the pictures where they look like a perfect angel, post the ones where they've just s**t down your arm! Show the truth. (Show the mothers-to-be what they're in for, haha!) Let's be ourselves.

### Likes, Not Dislikes

Why the f**k is there a 'dislike' button on YouTube anyway? I mean, how does that help anyone and why the hell do we need it? It's mad to think about it, really – the fact that we think it's OK to publicly tell someone we don't like what they've done. Like I said before, you can think it. but you really don't have to say it. So don't contribute to the hate online; even one little 'dislike' can make someone feel like crap. Let's not send out negative energy.

### Celebrate The Ordinary

Let's celebrate everyday brilliance on social media rather than only the people who do crazy stuff. Support the people doing great, everyday things like being a great friend, doing really well at school or work, helping someone in need or achieving something small and meaningful.

### Make Filters Fun

There are some really hilarious filters out there that make you look like random things (I mean, who came up with the idea of making our faces look like a frog, or a lemon?), and it can be so much fun swapping ridiculous pictures with our friends. Instead of chasing some kind of fake beauty 'ideal' with those filters that take away what makes us unique, let's use those different filters to have a laugh!

## My life on social media now

I've got a much better relationship with social media than I ever had before, but just like everyone else, once I'm on there, I get stuck scrolling! I don't have the urge to go on social media just to look at someone else's life — I'll only go on there to post myself — but then I can get locked on. My main reason to go online these days is to be in contact with my fans, and definitely one of the best elements about it for me is seeing people connect with my music. Aside from performing live, there's no real other way of seeing if I'm doing my job right. It's not like being a doctor, where if you make people better you know you've done well — my job doesn't work like that! So being able to see how much my music means to people online is really special.

I've also found that my Instagram captions have become a little bit of personal therapy for me. The way it works is I force myself to sit down and think about what I'm feeling, what my emotions are that day, and write it down. People might think I'm just trying to dole out advice but I'm actually talking to myself! I've got out a lot of emotional stuff this way.

*It's the power of letting things out, which is one of the biggest and most valuable lessons I've learned.*

One of my favourite things to do on my socials now is #TherapyIn15. I try to do it weekly on a Sunday, where everyone has just 15 minutes at 3 p.m. UK time to let out how they feel. A safe space. I also try to offer as good advice as I can. It first started years ago where it was called #AgonyAnne, then it turned into #SpeakYourMindin15mins and now it's #Therapyin15. It all comes from that idea of asking people how their week has been, so they have a chance to think about how things actually are, and get some problems off their chest. I also encourage anyone involved to help others out if they feel they can.

It's a small thing, but I hope that what I'm doing is working and helping people, and actually making a difference.

Through doing this, I've come to realise what my goal is in life: to make people feel better. It's a part of everything I do. I write songs for that reason, talking about subjects to help someone feel better about a situation they might be in, too. And with the online therapy, if I've helped someone get something off their chest, or be nicer to someone else in their lives, then that's amazing.

## Learning to unplug

I'm lucky I don't feel the need to ALWAYS be on my phone — I can put it away for a period of time and I love that! For me, it's exciting to occasionally remove my phone from my life. I can easily put it away for a morning or afternoon and not look at it at all. Honestly, when I do this, I feel more in the moment. I'm present (and actually feel like I remember things more easily!). Maybe it's a bit easier because being on my phone is part of my job now as an artist — I'm often on it because I have to be. If being on my phone was just a choice then maybe I wouldn't find it as easy, but I massively recommend it to everyone to do. Disconnecting from your phone every now and then is so good, and you know what? The world doesn't fall apart if you don't check social media every few minutes . . .

## Moving from reaction to compassion

If we all had empathy for each other, then we wouldn't have so much s**t going on in the world.

*Having compassion for other people alleviates so much stress and so many problems, for so many reasons.*

When I was an unhappy person, I found it really hard to move past my immediate, rage-y gut reactions on social media. I'd wanna lash out straight away. And if I read bad things about me, even just one comment, I couldn't help but take it on board. It would plant doubts in my head about myself, and send me into a downward spiral and I'd often be angry.

But like I said, I understand now that people are horrible on social media because they feel like s\*\*t themselves. So instead of retaliating, which is what I would have done, I'll take a breath and think about what they're going through in order to put something like that out there. It makes me feel for them instead, and view their comments from a more compassionate place. I just think: if everyone loved themselves, the world would be a better place because everyone would be kind. It's because people don't like themselves that they put out negativity.

Someone else who helped me shift my thinking was the artist and YouTuber KSI. We released a song together in 2021 called 'Don't Play', and one day I was with him as he looked through his social comments. I saw a few bad ones, and I couldn't help wondering how he didn't care about it, so I asked him. 'But it's hilarious, isn't it?' he said. 'It's funny that people think that, it's jokes.' His perspective was that it was totally entertaining that people who don't know you have these opinions about you. It made me see how irrelevant it all is. From that moment on, it felt good to laugh things off, like I had some protective coat around me.

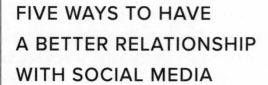

# FIVE WAYS TO HAVE A BETTER RELATIONSHIP WITH SOCIAL MEDIA

> Only go on when you want to post: don't just pick up your phone because you're bored

> Turn off the comments: it's not THE LAW that you have to read and absorb random people's random opinions

> Don't put your phone on the table when you're out: leave it in your bag or pocket and give your friends and family your proper attention

> Don't use it as your alarm clock: this way, you won't have it in your hand the second you wake up and see something that influences your mood

> Delete social media apps from your phone: Every now and then I delete apps for a time. It's so relaxing to have a little break from them. I found the app time limit thing doesn't really work, I just press ignore or 'remind me in 15 minutes' every 15 minutes.

## Fixing the social media disconnect

The reason I chose to keep the name Anne-Marie when I became an artist, rather than calling myself something else, was because it would let me be *me* as much as possible. That then gives me the chance to be my real self on social media.

I never felt a disconnect between 'me' and 'social media me'. I just post because I wanna post, and

*although I've made a few mistakes and learned a lot about how to treat social media, it's still my authentic self that I put out there.*

The reason I'm as real as I can be is that I know that people are watching, and I don't want it to be fake. But for so many people, there's a disconnect between who they really are in real life, and the persona they put out there on social media.

I'll give you an example. A few years ago I was doing promo and met two girls who were social media stars. We were all set up to record a video together, but when they came into the hotel to meet with me, they were really shy and hardly said a word. But as soon as they set up their phones to record the video, they were suddenly buzzing with energy and super confident. I was like, *S\*\*t!* They were completely different people for the cameras. It worried me; that disconnect between their true selves and their social selves.

I don't ever want to put something out there that isn't me. Look, I *could* post 'perfect' posts from now on, but WHY WOULD I? I don't want to portray that because 1, it's too much effort, 2, I don't actually look good all the time and 3, *it's not f\*\*king real life!*

Obviously, if you are having a great day, or you love your outfit or you just feel bad-ass and confident, post about it! One hundred per cent celebrate and share your happy days, but

*don't get caught in the habit of ONLY showing your best parts on social media. You'll get stuck in the trap of perfection,*

of pretending your life is completely flawless and this will just make everyone miserable, especially you. And, trust me, you deserve so much better than that.

If I could find a way
out of this hole /
I could do anything

# . . . One last thing from me

**W**hen we look at little kids, running about wearing messed-up clothes, being silly and un-self-conscious, laughing their heads off and jumping around playing games, what do we think of them? We don't laugh at them and think, *Oh they look so scruffy and stupid, how embarrassing.* Instead, we think the opposite, don't we? We see them as beautiful, happy and carefree. We look at them and smile.

Well, that's what I do anyway. I look at them with pure joy, happy that they're living every moment without any worries. They're content just to be themselves, it's amazing. And we were all like that, once.

Why does that have to change? I mean, I get growing up and taking responsibility for our lives and caring for our families and friends. That's important to learn. But I think in a lot of ways, we lose the positive stuff we knew inherently as children and instead, we take into adulthood a lot of negative things: anxiety, stress, self-consciousness, the list goes on.

## Rediscovering our inner joy

For me, so much of becoming a happier person has been about reconnecting with the things I loved as a child. Take being in nature, for instance. I was on holiday at a farm not long ago, and chatted to the person who ran it telling them thanks, how much I loved it there, and how I couldn't wait to come back. 'It's not me that you need to thank, I haven't done anything,' he said. 'It's the land that's giving you that energy and happiness. It's nature.'

He was right; ever since I was a tiny kid I've craved being in nature. I always wanted to be outdoors, playing in the park, or around trees in the forest. When I was a child I didn't have to think about *why*, I just knew it was something inside me – it's inside all of us. We crave it because we're part of nature, we're part of this planet. And having relearned how much I love it now, as an adult, has made me so much happier.

So I think we need to unlearn a lot of bad habits about growing up. To go back to that beauty of childhood, the happiness and joy we had naturally inside us. It was something one of those psychics in LA told me, too – not to forget my inner child. Because an amazing result from all the therapy I've had, and all the things I've learned, is that

*a huge part of my happiness was already inside me.*

The things that make me happy now were things that made me happy then. I just forgot how to access and enjoy them along the way into becoming a grown-up.

## We all have to look after our brains

Most of us understand we need to take care of our bodies to have a good, healthy life. Work out, eat well (have a lovely massage every now and then, maybe). That's accepted – that we have to look after our physical health. But why do we leave our brain behind? Why do we assume it can keep taking all the s**t we put in it? I mean, yes, our brains are really good at it. And they keep us together; functioning and understanding and bonding memories and making new connections every second. But our brain needs a break, too. And more than that, some care. A rest. Before it explodes! (Not literally, but you know what I mean . . .) A friend of mine gave me a really good analogy about this recently: if we went on a really long walk, we'd take breaks to rest our legs, wouldn't we? But we don't give our minds a break . . .

I never used to think about looking after my brain's health. I just didn't consider it as a thing! But it's our BRAIN, it's an organ. It's a bloody big one as well. So much is going on up there and it's working 24/7, every single day of our lives. Even when we're asleep! And we try to push it aside and say we're OK without looking after it, or considering our mental health at all? Hahahaha. Our mental health is our physical health. Look after every part of you. Don't leave your brain behind.

I'm fascinated by learning more about the science behind our brain; that's why I've got into reading more books recently and I love asking my therapist about what actually is going on when we feel a certain way. One fact that completely floors me is that in our conscious state we can process up to five thoughts at the same time, but also that we have around 60,000 thoughts per day.

I mean, *What the hell!* We have thousands of thoughts swirling around our brain that our subconscious is regulating for us without us even realising. It's keeping us safe, and alive, it's working insanely hard to help us stay as OK as we can be. And in return, we need to look after it by accepting that we ALL have mental health and we ALL need to look after it – it's not something that's scary and shameful.

For my whole life, until recently, I'd always thought of mental health as something totally separate to my brain. I thought it was something that was only associated with people who had real big obvious problems.

But it's not. Every doubt, every negative thought is our mental health telling us something. We all have that. It is to do with ALL OF US. The more we all start to understand and accept that, the better we'll all be.

## 'Therapy' is not a trigger word

Let's look at the word therapy. My friend Claire pointed out something really fascinating, which was that we all can talk about different types of 'therapy' that don't trigger us – like retail therapy, physiotherapy, hormone therapy. But the moment that we use it on its own – just 'therapy' – it becomes some scary word. So many people see it as a bad thing, and think if you have therapy it means you have massive problems and it's something to be ashamed of.

But I was thinking about this a while ago, and having therapy is like having a really good conversation with someone. At its best it's like chatting s**t with a great friend. It's there to help us understand ourselves better and make better lives for ourselves.

Someone else gave me a great analogy too, for how talking to someone helps us. Imagine your brain as a linen cupboard, and your thoughts and emotions are the towels and clothes inside it. Without talking and going over things, you're just throwing all the towels and clothes back inside every day and shutting the door quickly. But if you open it up again, everything will fall out. But when you do talk through your emotions, you're taking the time and care to fold each item properly, and put it back inside carefully. You're processing and looking after your thoughts so that things don't get messy and fall all over the place.

I've been lucky enough to be able to access therapy, and as you know, it has changed my life. But I also understand that it's not for everyone and often people aren't able to access therapy services. In this book I've explored lots of different ways that I hope you can help yourself, even if you can't have therapy. So let's start talking about it, as a word, as a thing, in a more positive way.

## Now it's over to you

Please know that if you've got to the end of this book, it doesn't mean that all your problems are fixed! (Neither are mine!) We are all works in progress.

*It's up to you now, to take these words and put them into action.*

I don't want this to be the last time you read this book either. You don't learn through reading things just once. Keep using it in the way that'll work best for you. Go back to certain sections that really spoke to you. Flick through it when you can. Make notes, highlight, make plans, change little habits, start new conversations. Write in this book, doodle some drawings, jot down notes, and share it online with me and use the hashtag #YouDeserveBetter so I can see them all. Speak about things to people in your life, share your emotions, don't pretend everything's OK when it's not.

Whatever it is, you just have to DO IT. Just reading along and nodding your head isn't enough. I've had to revisit a lot of these hard truths over the years to finally put it into action in my life.

I've shared my journey with you with the hope that it helps you with yours.

## Putting all the puzzle pieces together

In this book, I've talked about all the different parts of our lives, from body image, to career, to style, to self-care. And every single element is connected. We're not loads of separate things, working independently – it's not as if our career self is totally separate from our friendship self and they never affect each other. We're everything, we are all of these things and we're experiencing them all constantly. Life is messy.

*Every part of our life is a little piece of a jigsaw puzzle, and we only work well when the puzzle fits together.*

I hope by sharing my story, I've shown you how much all my experiences knit together. Being unhappy affected every part of my life, and working on myself has made every part of my life better. Sometimes I'm asked in interviews, 'When did you start being confident?' and I'm like, *I don't f\*\*king know!* I just know that it wasn't one 'thing' that made me confident, it was loads and loads of little interconnected changes that, over time, have made me a confident, happier, better person.

So, don't shut your feelings away. Cry if you want to, be angry if you want to, laugh if you want to. If you're struggling, it's f\*\*king hard to work on yourself and feel pain and sadness, but it is exactly these emotions that are a catalyst for change. And change is a beautiful thing.

You are enough. You are brilliant. You deserve better.

Thanks for reading my story. Now, it's your turn.

# Thank yous

I want to thank Orion – especially my publisher Ru – for trusting that my life story is interesting enough to put into book form. Ru, you have been so wonderful to work with, you believed in my vision and helped so much through this entire process. Becky, I am so grateful for all your time, energy and expertise you've shared with me during this process. I'm sorry for all the WhatsApps, but with each voice note and edit, we finally got there! Thank you to my lovely book agent, David Riding, for your guidance on a whole new world of publishing, and thank you to my lawyer, Nicky, for introducing us.

Thank you, Jazz, for just being the best manager and human. For making this happen and for re-introducing me to books and recommending many that have changed my life. I wouldn't have achieved what I have without you.

Thank you to my amazing therapist for helping me start living my life again. And listening to me chat s**t every week. You have made such a huge change in my life. Readers, I hope some of my learnings from her that I've shared in this book will also make your life better.

Thank you to my friends for bringing me joy; I am so lucky to have you. It was so much fun being able to write about you all. To all the friends mentioned in this book, thank you for always supporting me through my ups and downs.

Love always to my family for being so supportive of everything I do.

My family approach everything with kindness and an open mind – things I love about them hugely. Mum, dad, grandad and Sam – I love you all so much.

Thank you to the music industry community for accepting me and helping and pushing for my success. It's been a long journey to get here but I feel so much more at ease with everything I do now. Being championed and respected by my peers within the industry is the best of feelings!

I'd like to say a huge thank you to every brand I've worked with and TV show I've ever been on. Thank you for believing in me and pushing me forward. Even after all this time it is still so amazing. To every radio DJ that has ever championed me and played my music – THANK YOU! I still LOVE it whenever I hear one of my songs on the radio . . . it will never get old!

Thank you to every single person who I've met in my life. You have changed me in some way, for the better without even knowing. I just feel so lucky. Lucky to be here, to be alive, to be able to tell you my story. Finally, thank YOU for picking up this book.

Love,
Anne-Marie xx

## About the author

Anne-Marie's rise to stardom has been nothing short of meteoric. A former three-time karate World Champion and West End child star turned multi-platinum-selling artist, Anne-Marie has grown to become one of the world's most-loved and successful pop stars.

Following a string of chart-busting singles over her career to date, including her UK Top 3 '2002', Anne-Marie's 2018 debut album, *Speak Your Mind*, was the biggest-selling debut release of that year in the UK, and has sold over four million copies across the world.

Making her prime time debut as a new, and winning, coach on talent show *The Voice* this year, nine-time BRIT Award nominee Anne-Marie also recently released her much-anticipated second studio album, *Therapy*. An album title that holds an extremely important message to the Mind charity ambassador, Anne-Marie continues to campaign for the conversation surrounding mental health.

*You Deserve Better* is Anne-Marie's first book.